BRIGHT NOTES

SONS AND LOVERS AND OTHER WORKS BY D. H. LAWRENCE

Intelligent Education

Nashville, Tennessee

BRIGHT NOTES: Sons and Lovers and Other Works
www.BrightNotes.com

No part of this publication may be used or reproduced in any manner whatsoever without written permission, except in the case of brief quotations in critical articles and reviews. For permissions, contact Influence Publishers http://www.influencepublishers.com.

ISBN: 978-1-645420-80-4 (Paperback)
ISBN: 978-1-645420-81-1 (eBook)

Published in accordance with the U.S. Copyright Office Orphan Works and Mass Digitization report of the register of copyrights, June 2015.

Originally published by Monarch Press.
Sandra M. Gilbert, 1965
2020 Edition published by Influence Publishers.

Interior design by Lapiz Digital Services. Cover Design by Thinkpen Designs.

Printed in the United States of America.

Library of Congress Cataloging-in-Publication Data forthcoming.
Names: Intelligent Education
Title: BRIGHT NOTES: Sons and Lovers and Other Works
Subject: STU004000 STUDY AIDS / Book Notes

CONTENTS

1) Introduction to D. H. Lawrence — 1

2) Textual Analysis — 11
   - Part I: Chapters 1 - 3 — 11
   - Part I: Chapters 4 - 6 — 25
   - Part II: Chapters 7 - 11 — 37
   - Part II: Chapters 12 - 15 — 57

3) Character Analyses — 73

4) Critical Commentary — 83

5) The Rainbow — 89

6) Women in Love — 93

7) The Plumed Serpent — 97

8) Essay Questions and Answers — 101

9) Subject Bibliography and Guide to Research Papers — 110

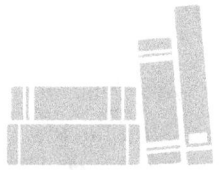

INTRODUCTION TO D. H. LAWRENCE

CHILDHOOD AND YOUTH

D. H. Lawrence was born in 1885 in Eastwood - the Bestwood of *Sons and Lovers* - a mining town just outside Nottingham, in the industrial Midlands of England. Like Paul Morel, he was the son of a coal miner, Arthur Lawrence, and a strong - willed, refined, middle - class girl, Lydia Beardsall Lawrence, formerly a schoolteacher, who, like Gertrude Morel, had married "beneath her." In fact, the picture of Paul's childhood given in *Sons and Lovers* is as accurate and detailed a picture of Lawrence's own boyhood as any biographer conceivably could draw. Unlike Paul, Lawrence had two older brothers, an older sister and a younger sister (Ada, who was to be the family member closest to him after his mother's death), but there the differences end. Like Paul, Lawrence was quiet, "good," rather religious as a boy and intensely attached to his mother. Like Walter and Gertrude Morel, Arthur and Lydia Lawrence fought constantly and, to a child, frighteningly. Arthur Lawrence drank, like Walter Morel, and his children hated him, as the Morel children hate their father. Like Paul Morel, Lawrence early began to paint and to exhibit other signs of creativity and extraordinary intelligence. And like Paul, also, "Bert" Lawrence fell in love with a nearby farm, the Haggs (called Willey Farm in *Sons and Lovers*) and half in love with the girl who lived on it, Jessie Chambers, who became the Miriam of *Sons and Lovers*.

MIRIAM

In real life, Lawrence's relationship with Jessie was almost exactly that of Paul and Miriam in *Sons and Lovers*. Indeed, Jessie Chambers herself contributed her own recollections of this early and intense relationship to the manuscript originally called Paul Morel, in the form of a number of individual narrations which Lawrence, of course, rewrote and revised, but many of whose central facts and points were certainly incorporated into the book. Like Miriam, Jessie was an intense, "spiritual" girl who loved the brilliant young writer with an almost religious fervor. Lawrence, for his part, was quite as dependent on Jessie's judgments and on her encouragement as Paul is on Miriam, and Lydia Lawrence, the writer's mother, felt the same unyielding hostility toward Jessie that Mrs. Morel feels for Miriam. And like Gertrude Morel, Lydia Lawrence finally defeated the girl Jessie in their silent struggle for Lawrence's love. In fact, a day or two after his mother died, Lawrence took Jessie for a walk and told her "You know, J., I've always loved mother." "I know you have," she replied. "I don't mean that," he answered. "I've loved her - like a lover - that's why I could never love you."

BEGINNINGS OF TWO CAREERS

When Lawrence was twelve, like Arthur and not Paul Morel, he won a scholarship to Nottingham High School, but unlike Arthur he remained at home, commuting from Eastwood to Nottingham daily. After High School, again unlike Paul, he went to work for several years as an uncertified teacher in

Eastwood and nearby Ilkeston (like Ursula Brangwen, in *The Rainbow*) and then (again like Ursula) he went on to take a two year teacher - training course at the University of Nottingham. After completing it, in 1908, Lawrence was appointed as a regular teacher at the Davidson Road School in the London suburb of Croydon. At around this time, however, his "second" - his major - career, as a writer, began, for although he had won several short story prizes as an undergraduate at Nottingham he had until now made no effort to publish seriously. In 1909, though, Jessie Chambers sent some of his poems to Ford Madox Ford, then the editor of *The English Review*, and Ford, immediately enthusiastic, printed them in the lead spot in the magazine's November issue. Ford, who enjoyed "discovering" and encouraging young writers, was easily convinced that Lawrence was a genius, and through his influence the twenty - four - year old author had his first novel quickly accepted by the London publishing company of Heinemann, Ltd. *The White Peacock*, which Lawrence later called "a florid prose - poem," was certainly no masterpiece. But despite its many faults - it was over - written and pretentious - its creator's genius shone through, and with its publication one of the chief literary careers of this century was launched.

TRAGEDY AND THE TRESPASSER

Triumph though the publication of *The White Peacock* might have been for Lawrence, his satisfaction was short - lived, for the book was barely out when his adored mother became mortally ill and died of cancer on December 9, 1910. Within a year after her death, overwhelmed by grief and illness, Lawrence gave up teaching and went back to Eastwood to recuperate. In the meantime he had been working on his second novel, *The Trespasser* (which he later called "a decorated idyll running to seed in **realism**") and it was published in 1912, to a rather mixed critical reception.

FRIEDA

Lawrence was now pretty much at loose ends. Convinced that strenuous teaching of the Croydon sort was undermining his health, he went to see his old French teacher at Nottingham University, Professor Ernest Weekley, in the hope that Weekley might get him a post as an English "Lektor" in a German University. But at Weekley's house, Lawrence - who had all this while been carrying on a number of intense but none too satisfactory romantic affairs - met "the woman of a lifetime." Frieda Weekley, the Professor's thirty - two - year - old German wife. Married for twelve years to this English academic and the mother of three children, Frieda was the daughter of a German aristocrat, Baron von Richthofen, and up until this fateful meeting with Lawrence, she later related, her adult life had been passed in a kind of domestic half - sleep. But Lawrence, like the "Prince Charming" figure who awakens the "Sleeping Beauty" in so many of his later tales and stories, brought Frieda emphatically back to life and wakefulness. The two quickly fell in love and, painful as it was for Frieda to abandon her children, they decided to leave the country together. After many ups and downs they finally began their new life in Germany, in May of 1912, and two years later, in 1914, Frieda managed to obtain a divorce from Ernest Weekley so that she might actually marry Lawrence, which she did on July 13 of that year. Like many great men, Lawrence was utterly dependent on his wife for his emotional well - being. Though he and Frieda had many very well - publicized fights, their relationship was one of complete honesty, intimacy and love. Frieda tempered many of Lawrence's more extravagant flights of fancy, and much of his mystical earnestness, with her teutonic common sense, her womanly shrewdness and her earthy wit. And Lawrence, whose "gift for life" was unsurpassed, continually opened the doors of perception and experience for her, as she so often testified.

SONS AND LOVERS

Sons and Lovers was begun shortly after Lydia Lawrence's death in 1910, when Lawrence was staying in Eastwood. His first partial draft of the novel, according to Jessie Chambers, was "flat and tepid," with a melodramatic and over - contrived plot. But at Jessie's suggestion he revised his plan for the book, converting it into a more accurate and detailed record of his actual boyhood experiences. In this, as we have already seen, he was substantially aided by Jessie herself, who even supplied narratives of her own for him to work from. Later, when he and Frieda were "honeymooning" in Germany, Lawrence took up the book once more, and with Frieda providing "bits" as Jessie once had (especially those dealing with the mother's reaction) plus some helpful letters from Jessie herself, he finally completed this first masterpiece of his.

LAWRENCE'S PLAN OF THE BOOK

In a letter to Edward Garnett, who had by now taken the place of Ford as the young novelist's editor and mentor, Lawrence outlined his plan of *Sons and Lovers* in what is perhaps one of the clearest and most succinct summaries of a book ever provided by its author:

. . . a woman of character and refinement goes into the lower class, and has no satisfaction in her own life. She has had a passion for her husband, so the children are born of passion, and have heaps of vitality. But as her sons grow up she selects them as lovers - first the eldest, then the second. These sons are urged into life by their reciprocal love of their mother - urged on and on. But when they come to manhood, they can't love, because their mother is the strongest power in their lives, and holds them. . . . As soon as the young men come into contact with women, there's a split. William gives his sex to a fribble, and his mother holds his soul. But the split kills him, because he doesn't know where he is. The next son gets a woman who fights for his soul - fights his mother. The son loves the mother - all the sons hate and are jealous of the father. The battle goes on between the mother and the girl, with the son as object. The mother gradually proves stronger, because of the tie of blood. The son decides to leave his soul in his mother's hands, and, like his elder brother, go for passion. He gets passion. Then the split begins to tell again. But, almost unconsciously, the mother realizes what is the matter, and begins to die. The son casts off his mistress, attends to his mother dying. He is left in the end naked of everything, with the drift towards death.

Of course, many critics have pointed out that Lawrence was not quite honest with himself in this prospectus - and that in certain respects he was actually inaccurate. Seymour Betsky, for instance, remarks that "Lawrence's own words become **irony** in reverse. He misleads. To say that 'the mother proves stronger because of the tie of blood' is to call attention away from the manner in which the novel itself builds up cumulatively the more formidable impression of her strength of character. The 'tie of blood' is by far the subordinate impression. . . . Further, Lawrence positively errs. It is clear that the 'drift towards death' contradicts the ending of the novel." Nevertheless, despite its flaws, most readers would agree that Lawrence's statement is for the most part remarkably sure and clear, and that the author fulfilled his plan remarkably well in the novel itself.

FREUD AND SONS AND LOVERS

As Graham Hough has pointed out, "the whole situation (of *Sons and Lovers*) presents the Freudian Oedipal imbroglio in almost classic completeness," which, of course, raises the question of Lawrence's familiarity with Freud at the time of its writing in 1912. Actually, we now know pretty certainly that Lawrence had not read Freud at all when he wrote this book, but - and this is a very important "but" indeed - Frieda Lawrence writes in her memoir, *Not I But The Wind*, that before her first meeting with Lawrence she "had met a remarkable disciple of Freud and was full of undigested theories." In the course of their first conversation she and Lawrence "talked about Oedipus and understanding leaped through our words." Later, according to Hough, "she wrote that she was a great admirer of Freud when she met Lawrence in 1912, and that he and she had long arguments about Freud together." "And of course," Hough adds, "the final draft of *Sons and Lovers* was written as strongly under Frieda's influence as the earlier ones had been under Miriam's [Jessie's]. *Sons and Lovers* is indeed the first Freudian novel in English, but its Freudianism is mediated not by a text - book but by a person...."

LAWRENCE'S LATER NOVELS

After *Sons and Lovers* Lawrence produced, in pretty rapid succession, the two books which are generally considered (cf. the Critical Commentary) his greatest works - *The Rainbow* (completed in 1915) and *Women in Love* (finished in 1916). But though *The Rainbow* was published in September of 1915, it was suppressed because of its sexual frankness by November of that year, and Lawrence could not find a publisher for *Women in Love* until 1920, when it was published privately in New York. His other later novels include *The Lost Girl* (published 1920), *The Plumed Serpent* (published 1926) and *Lady Chatterley's Lover* (published 1928, in Florence).

OTHER WORK

In addition to his novels, which are generally considered his major work as a writer, Lawrence also produced a good deal of criticism, several plays, some wonderful travel books, and a considerable body of poetry which, though uneven, contains some of the finest poems to be written by an Englishman in this century. A complete list of Lawrence's works is given in the bibliography, but the most notable among them include *Fantasia of the Unconscious* (published 1922) - a fascinating statement of Lawrence's occasionally muddled but often incisive philosophy of life; *Studies in Classic American Literature* (published 1923) - a trailblazing study of American writers, which has become a classic in its own right; *Birds, Beasts and Flowers* (published 1923) - a brilliant volume of nature poems, equal in acuteness of observation and lyric intensity to the best modern poetry; and the travel volumes *Twilight in Italy* (published 1916), *Sea and Sardinia* (published 1921), M*ornings in Mexico* (published 1927) and *Etruscan Places* (published posthumously, 1932), which probably contain the finest travel writing to have been produced so far in this century.

LAST ILLNESS AND DEATH

After his new life with Frieda began, Lawrence led a nomadic, restless, rootless existence. A complete record of his and

Frieda's wanderings would be too complicated to detail here, and the interested reader is referred to *Poste Restante: A D. H. Lawrence Travel Calendar* by Harry T. Moore, or to Mr. Moore's excellent biography, *The Intelligent Heart*. While he was in Mexico, in 1925 (where he wrote *The Plumed Serpent*, which deals with that country), Lawrence became dangerously ill with "malaria" and with a lung infection, which subsequently turned out to be tuberculosis. He had always been delicate and, since childhood, subject to terrible bouts of acute bronchitis and pneumonia, which might have killed a man less vividly alive and less tenacious of life. In the years between 1925 and 1929, though he and Frieda continued to travel as extensively as before, Lawrence's condition gradually worsened until, by the winter of 1929, which they spent at Bandol, on the Riviera, for the sake of Lawrence's health, it was clear that he was a dying man. Two of his most magnificent poems were written at this time, dealing clear - sightedly and profoundly with the subject of death - "Bavarian Gentians" and "The Ship of Death" - for Lawrence was essentially a religious man, who felt an urgent need to come to terms with the mystery that was about to overtake him. Always spiritually vigorous, he continued to write up to the very end with his powers undiminished and his mind unimpaired. The most moving account of his death in 1930 has been given by Frieda Lawrence herself:

After lunch he began to suffer very much and about tea - time he said: "I must have a temperature, I am delirious. Give me the thermometer." This is the only time, seeing his tortured face, that I cried, and he said: "Don't cry," in a quick, compelling voice ... [later] he said: "Hold me, hold me, I don't know where I am, I don't know where my hands are ... where am I?" Then the doctor came and gave him a morphine injection.... The minutes went by.... I held his left ankle from time to time, it felt so full of life, all my days I shall hold his ankle in my hand. He was breathing more peacefully, and then suddenly there were gaps in the breathing. The moment came when the thread of life tore in his heaving chest, his face changed, his cheeks and jaw sank, and death had taken hold of him . . . we buried him, very simply, like a bird we put him away, a few of us who loved him. We put flowers into his grave and all I said was: 'Good - bye Lorenzo,' as his friends and I put lots and lots of mimosa on his coffin.

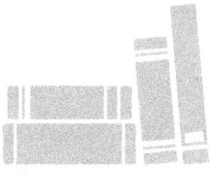

SONS AND LOVERS

TEXTUAL ANALYSIS

PART I: CHAPTERS 1 - 3

CHAPTER ONE: THE EARLY MARRIED LIFE OF THE MORELS

Sons and Lovers opens with a description of The Bottoms, a meagre residential development built for the workers' families by the mining company of Carston, Waite & Co. in the great grimy coal and iron field of Nottinghamshire and Derbyshire. The Bottoms consists of "six blocks of miners' dwellings, two rows of three, like the dots on a blank - six domino, and twelve houses in a block." From the outside the houses seem quite "substantial and very decent," and in front there are pretty gardens. But the real life of the houses goes on in the kitchens, which open onto a long common alley lined with ash - pits (garbage dumps). "So," Lawrence points out, "the actual conditions of living in the Bottoms ... were quite unsavoury."

When the story begins, Mrs. Gertrude Morel, one of the two principal characters, is about seven months pregnant. She is a small, slight woman of thirty-one, who already has a seven-year-old son, William, and a five-year-old daughter, Annie. She has only recently moved to the Bottoms from the neighboring village of Bestwood, and she still shrinks a little from contact with the rather vulgar Bottoms women. She herself is obviously a finer type.

On this particular July day, Mrs. Morel's son William is pestering his mother for twopence with which to go to the fair which has just opened nearby. Annie, too, is begging to be taken there. Heavy with child and weary as she is, Mrs. Morel trudges up the hill to the fairgrounds. Her children are delighted by all the wonderful attractions, and proud of their genteel-looking mother, too. Their father is "helping out" at a nearby tavern, but in any case he is a hard drinker with little interest in his family.

Mrs. Morel's life in The Bottoms is a difficult one, we soon learn. Her marriage is obviously not happy. She despises her brutish, hard-drinking, coal-miner husband, and she is "sick of ... the struggle with poverty and ugliness and meanness" that is their life. "Looking ahead, the prospect of her life" makes her "feel as if she were buried alive." Her carefree girlhood now seems far away indeed. Originally she "came of a good old burgher family, famous independents who had fought with Colonel Hutchinson and who remained stout Congregationalists." Her grandfather was a lace-manufacturer ruined at a time when many others also failed in the Nottingham lace business. Her father was a "handsome, haughty man," an engineer.

As a girl, Gertrude Morel had had a "young man" - an educated, charming boy named John Field. But when his father's business failed, young Field went off to become a teacher and later married a wealthy widow. Mrs. Morel never forgot - and perhaps never forgave - him. Later, when she was twenty-three, she met Walter Morel at a Christmas party. He was a healthy, good-looking young miner of twenty-seven, with "a vigorous black beard that had never been shaved." Though he was uneducated and a common man, Morel had a curious animal attraction for the proud, reserved, intellectual Gertrude. He loved to dance and flirt; "he was so ready and pleasant with everybody." She, on the other hand, was to him "that thing of mystery and fascination, a lady." Within a year they were married.

For three months after marrying Walter Morel Gertrude Morel was "perfectly happy: for six months she was very happy." After that, disillusionment set in. Gertrude discovered that the house they lived in, which she thought Walter owned, was actually his mother's property and that he was paying the older woman an exorbitant rent. Furthermore, he was deeply in debt for their furniture, which his wife had thought was already paid for. Not only that, he had been stopping off at pubs for a pint after work, a habit which outraged Mrs. Morel more than any of his other offenses, for she is a teetotaller who forced her husband to sign "the pledge" when she married him. At this point, Lawrence tells us, "there began a battle between the husband and wife - a fearful, bloody battle that ended only with the death of one. She fought to make him undertake his own responsibilities, to make him fulfill his obligations. But he was too different from her. His nature was purely sensuous, and she strove to make him moral, religious." And it was amid the smoke of this battle, as it were, that the Morel children grew up.

The coming of children aggravated the already existing tension between their parents. By the time young William was born, Mrs. Morel had been disillusioned by her husband, and she determined to live for her son: he was all that she cared for in the world. When he was a year old, Morel tried to surprise her by crudely cutting the child's hair. "Yer non want ter make a wench on 'un," he explains. But Gertrude never forgave him for "this act of masculine clumsiness" which "was the spear through the side of her love for" him.

As the couple's marriage disintegrates, Walter Morel's drinking becomes worse. Often he drinks up half his wages, leaving his wife with major household debts unpaid, and no means to pay them. At the time of the fair, Mrs. Morel, who is strenuously saving to help pay the extra expenses of the new baby, is especially bitter that Morel has gone off cavorting with friends, leaving neither time nor money for his family. When he comes home that night, she reproaches him for his drinking, and he, in a rage, orders her out of the house. Though she refuses to go ("I've got those children to see to," she cries), he pushes her roughly out the door, locks it behind her and falls into a drunken stupor. She walks in the garden awhile, but soon, cold and tired, tries to come in again. Morel is oblivious to her taps and knocks. It takes her an hour to wake him, and when he finally lets her back in again, he disappears guiltily upstairs, without a word of apology.

Comment

This first chapter provides important background material, without which the central relationships of *Sons and Lovers* would be much harder to understand. Gertrude Morel, one of the novel's main characters, is a "refined," strong - willed, intelligent, ambitious woman, trapped in an unsuitable marriage. Her puritanical aversion to drinking and dancing is exactly the opposite of the high - spirited, easy - going Morel's delight in such earthly pleasures. Her bourgeois detestation of debts and deficits is foreign to her more relaxed, lower - class husband. Her marriage to him seems to have been one of life's accidents, like her father's business failure and John Field's father's failure. "Sometimes life takes hold of one," Lawrence writes, "carries the body along, accomplishes one's history, and yet is not real, but leaves oneself as it were slurred over." So it seems to Mrs. Morel, for certainly her grubby life in The Bottoms doesn't seem in any sense related to her own character. The vulgarity and coarseness of the common life along the alley of ash pits seems to have nothing to do with the spiritual aspirations, the lightness and quick - mindedness, of the young Gertrude Morel. "I wait," Mrs. Morel says to herself, "I wait, and what I wait for can never come." In this respect, she reminds us of the heroine of another realistic novel, Madame Bovary. Only Emma Bovary is finally to find fulfillment - or imagine she has found it - in the relationships with her lovers, while Gertrude Morel finds her fulfillment in her children.

The central relationship depicted in this chapter, however, is not yet that of Mrs. Morel and her children (especially her sons) but still the agonized, misshapen relationship of Mrs. Morel and her husband. Their long conflict, that "fearful, bloody battle that ended only with the death of one," is, after all, one of the crucial conflicts of the book, and certainly it is the one conflict that triggers all the others, for if Mrs. Morel's marriage were satisfactory she wouldn't need to use her children as she does.

Interestingly, as we shall see in our examination of some of Lawrence's later novels, this kind of sexual, man - woman battle is a central, perpetually recurring preoccupation in Lawrence's work, and we might indeed expect it to be, for *Sons and Lovers* is an autobiographical novel which depicts the relationship between Lawrence's own parents, a relationship which obviously determined the author's later view of the world.

The class difference between Mr. and Mrs. Morel - the refined, middle - class girl, and the lower -class miner - is another situation that recurs often in Lawrence's writing, a variant of what Harry T. Moore has called the "Sleeping Beauty theme," in which a man, often of low birth, perhaps a servant or gypsy (or miner) awakens or (as here) tries to awaken the sexuality of a higher - born lady. Indeed, as Moore's phrase implies, in his later, less realistic work Lawrence often used this sort of relationship in a fairy - tale kind of way. *Lady Chatterley's Lover*, in which the lowly gamekeeper awakens the sexuality of the lady of the manor, is a case in point, for Mellors is a natural development of Walter Morel. By the time he wrote *Lady Chatterley*, however, as Moore points out, Lawrence's sympathies were more with the dynamic figure of his father than (as earlier) with the refined mother figure. He realized that when he was young he had seen his exuberant, sensual father largely through a distorted glass supplied by his puritanical mother. But at the time he wrote *Sons and Lovers* Lawrence was still "on his mother's side," as it were, and he tended, at least in part, to portray the mother - figure, Mrs. Morel, as self - sacrificing and angelic while the father, Mr. Morel, was coarse, brutish and ignoble.

As we shall see, however, Lawrence was too skillful a novelist to create characters who were simply black and white, all - good or all - bad figures. Much of the later conflict in the book will, in fact, result from the tension between what is unselfish and what is selfish in Mrs. Morel, between her nurturing and her stifling of her sons. Similarly, there will always be some (though a little less) tension between Mr. Morel's irresponsible drunkenness and his animal magnetism, which Lawrence, often in spite of himself, conveys so clearly to the reader.

CHAPTER TWO: THE BIRTH OF PAUL AND ANOTHER BATTLE

After the scene with his wife which concluded the last chapter, Walter Morel feels guilty and tries to make it up to Gertrude by staying home and doing little jobs around the house for her. He even brings her morning tea in bed. But his clumsy presence irritates her, and the two soon lapse back into their old relationship. On the day when Paul - the expected baby - is born, Morel is in an especially bad mood. His work in the pit has gone poorly, and he comes home cross and tired. When he's told that his wife has been delivered of a son, he just grunts and sits down to his dinner. He's still cross later on, because of the disruption in his usual routine: the midwife gave him dinner on the wrong size plate and didn't build a large enough fire. After dinner "he went reluctantly upstairs. It was a struggle to face his wife at this moment, and he was tired. His face was black, and smeared with sweat . . . he stood at the foot of the bed.

'Well, how are ter, then?' he asked.

'I s'll be all right,' she answered.

'H'm!'

He stood at a loss what to say next. He was tired, and this bother was rather a nuisance to him. . . .

'A lad, tha says,' he stammered.

She turned down the sheet and showed the child.

'Bless him!' he murmured. Which made her laugh, because he blessed by rote - pretending paternal emotion, which he did not feel just then. . . . Dismissed, he wanted to kiss her, but he dared not. She half wanted him to kiss her, but could not bring herself to give any sign."

During this period, Mrs. Morel receives daily visits from a young Congregational minister, a widower. She is fond of him, and he, for his part, "depended on her. For hours, he talked to her, when she was well. He became the godparent of the child." One time, while he and Mrs. Morel are having tea, Morel comes home early. Flushed with work, sweaty and grimy from the mine, he bullies the poor, shy young clergyman and treats his wife roughly in the man's presence. Mrs. Morel and the children are especially annoyed by the scene because "whenever he had an audience, he [Morel] whined and played for sympathy. William . . . hated him, with a boy's hatred for false sentiment, and for the stupid treatment of his mother. Annie had never liked him; she merely avoided him."

One night, just after the young parson has left, Mrs. Morel goes for a walk in the fields with Annie and the new baby. As she sits under the trees in the meadow, drinking in the peace of the scene around her, she feels "strangely" towards the baby who is playing on her knee. He seems to knit his brow as though he is in pain. "He looks as if he was thinking about something - quite sorrowful," Mrs. Morel's next - door neighbor, Mrs. Kirk, has told her. And after all, Mrs. Morel reflects, she had not really wanted this child. "She no longer loved her husband; she had not wanted this child to come, and there it lay in her arms and pulled at her heart. . . . A wave of hot love went over her to the infant. She held it close to her face and breast. With all her force, with all her soul she would make up to it for having brought it into the world unloved. She would love it all the more, now it was here; carry it in her love. . . . 'I will call him "Paul,"' she said suddenly; she knew not why."

At home, things go as badly as ever between the Morels. One night shortly after her experience in the meadow, Mrs. Morel is waiting up late when her husband comes home, drunk and staggering. When she ignores his demands for food, he becomes enraged, and in the course of their quarrel he hurls a kitchen drawer at her. She has been sitting in her rocker by the fire, nursing the baby, and the drawer catches her over the eye, badly cutting her left temple, but fortunately the child is unhurt. Shocked into some semblance of sobriety, Morel tries to apologize and to help his wife bandage her brow. But she rejects him coldly. The next morning neither talks to the other, nor does Morel make any further efforts to apologize. Mrs. Morel "would have felt sorry for him," Lawrence tells us, "if he had once said, 'Wife, I'm sorry.' But no, he insisted to himself it was her fault." Before the week is out, Morel has spent so much money on drink that he is obliged to steal sixpence from his wife's purse in order to go to the tavern again. But when Mrs. Morel accuses him of this action, he denies it bitterly. In fact, he's so angry that he swears he will leave her. He packs a large bundle full of his belongings, and as the children wail in the corner, wondering what will become of them without his support, he stalks out in a rage. But Mrs. Morel knows that he won't go far. "One part of her said, it would be a relief to see the last of him; another part fretted because of keeping the children; and inside her, as yet, she could not quite let him go. At the bottom, she knew very well he could not go." And, indeed, go he does not. Outside, Mrs. Morel finds his bundle, ignominiously deposited in a corner of the garden. Walter and Gertrude Morel are inextricably involved with each other, eternally tied together by powerful bonds of hatred and dying love.

Comment

In this chapter the character of Walter Morel is delineated more fully. As we see in his treatment of the young clergyman, Morel is a bully and, so Lawrence tells us, a whiner. Perhaps, the author implies, his brutishness and drunkenness might even have been forgiven by his children; but he can never be forgiven for indulging in the kind of maudlin sentimentality which is so repellent to children.

His reaction to his new son, Paul, might also be forgiven - how many fathers, after all, feel a great surge of paternal love with the birth of every child? - were it not for his lack of consideration for his wife. And finally, even his drunken rages might be forgiven by the children and by Mrs. Morel if he had the compassion and the humility to apologize to his wife for his action. Instead Morel, proud and sullen, sulks and drinks some more after wounding Mrs. Morel in the head, and then commits what is to the bourgeois Mrs. Morel perhaps the greatest sin - stealing her grocery money to pay for further drinking.

Nevertheless we see in this chapter that, as in all the violent male - female relationships which Lawrence explored in fiction, Walter and Gertrude Morel are still profoundly dependent on each other. They hate each other; they fight furiously; yet Walter cannot leave his wife, when she challenges him to do so. And, deep inside, his wife does not yet want him to leave her either. This relationship, which was originally based on a powerful sexual attraction between two totally different people, still retains elements of that first magnetism (as, for instance, in the couple's momentary yearning toward each other after the birth of Paul). The hatred and violence which has grown up between the Morels in recent years still cannot entirely eradicate the basic need that drove them together in the beginning. And it is in this atmosphere of ambivalent hostility that the Morel children are to be raised.

Of course, despite the emphasis here on enriching the portrait of Walter Morel, the most important event in Chapter Two is the birth of Paul Morel, the central character of *Sons and Lovers*. *Sons and Lovers* is, after all, a classic bildungsroman (literally, in German, a "development novel"), a type of novel which deals with the formation and growth to maturity of one individual, usually a sensitive or artistic person who is shaped, before the reader's eyes, into a talented (and often disturbed) adult by the various forces which act on him throughout his childhood and youth. Thus it is profoundly significant for the novel as a whole that Paul Morel is born into this electric, thunderstorm atmosphere of hatred and passion; that his mother doesn't want him until after he is born; that his father greets his arrival with indifference and self-indulgence; and, perhaps most important, that his mother is driven, by guilt and loneliness and despair, to clasp the child to her with extra intensity, as if by living for him and through him she can make up to him (and to herself) for the violent and sordid home in which he must grow up.

CHAPTER THREE: THE CASTING OFF OF MOREL - THE TAKING ON OF WILLIAM

Gradually, despite the small tenderness and the residual passion between them, the Morels drift apart. Shortly after the last big fight, when he'd walked out on her, Walter Morel falls ill. Like many miners, Lawrence tells us, Morel loves to dose himself with various herbal infusions, but this time they do him no good. He is desperately sick with inflammation of the brain. His wife is utterly taken up with nursing him, and if the neighbors were not kind enough to help with the housework and the children, she would be too exhausted to go on. "Nevertheless," we learn, "there was a state of peace in the house for some time. Mrs. Morel was more tolerant of him, and he, depending on her almost like a child, was rather happy. Neither knew that she was more tolerant because she loved him less."

While Morel is convalescing from his illness, the truce between him and his wife continues. Mrs. Morel even conceives again, and the baby is another boy, Arthur, a beautiful child with golden curls, who turns out to be surprisingly attached to his father. Mrs. Morel's emotions, however, are slowly, inexorably shifting from her husband to her children. "Henceforward [Morel] was more or less a husk. And he half acquiesced, as so many men do, yielding their place to their children."

At this point Lawrence, too, shifts his attention from the parents to the children. We learn that Paul is a delicate, strange child, given to inexplicable crying jags. "These fits were not often, but they caused a shadow in Mrs. Morel's heart, and her treatment of Paul was different from that of the other children." William, the oldest, is still her favorite, however. One time when a neighbor complains to the Morels that William has torn her son's shirt in a fight, Mrs. Morel only mildly reprimands her son, while accepting his explanation of the event, but later, when Mr. Morel comes home and wants to beat the boy, she rushes between father and son, in a fury. "Only dare," she cries, "Only dare, milord, to lay a finger on that child! You'll regret it forever." And her husband is afraid of her - afraid enough to turn away and leave William alone.

When the children are old enough to be left unattended, Mrs. Morel joins the Women's Guild, a local women's club devoted to social discussion and mental improvement. The children are proud of their mother's quick mind and her intellectual activities.

Much as they love her and want her undivided attention, they never begrudge her this outside interest.

When William is thirteen, his mother gets him a job as a clerk, though his father had wanted him to go into the mines, as he himself did. The lad, handsome, alert and athletic, progresses rapidly at his work. He also goes to night school, "so that by the time he was sixteen he was the best shorthand clerk and bookkeeper in the place, except one!" In the meantime, he has also begun to go out with girls. He loves dancing and parties and is very popular. Naturally, his mother disapproves. Partly, she is jealous of his girlfriends but even more strongly, she is "afraid of her son's going the same way as his father."

At nineteen, William gets a job in Nottingham, the nearest city, which pays twice what his old job in Bestwood had. The other children are doing well at school: Annie is studying to be a teacher, and Paul and Arthur are excellent students. Then, after a year in Nottingham, William is offered a good job in London, at the "fabulous" salary of one hundred twenty pounds a year. His mother is miserable at the impending separation from him, but "it never occurred to him that she might be more hurt at his going away than glad of his success." A few days before he leaves, William burns all his love letters - he has quite a collection of them, having been exceedingly popular with the local girls - and as his mother looks on, disapproving, he gives the little decorative borders of the pages to his younger brother, Paul. "And William went to London, to start a new file."

Comment

In this chapter, Lawrence's emphasis has finally shifted from the Morels to their children. The battle between the parents, which forms so important a part of the Morel family's life, has been established and delineated; now it is relegated to the background - the background both of the children's lives and of Lawrence's novel - an important but partly submerged fact in the family's history.

The children, who seem so far to have turned out quite well, now take their properly central place in the narrative. William, Mrs. Morel's first love among them, is a handsome intelligent boy who combines his father's gregariousness with his mother's intellect. He seems destined for success. But even this early in his picture of the young family, Lawrence introduces two facts which are to become increasingly significant. One is Mrs. Morel's fear of William's social life, especially her dislike and jealousy of his girlfriends. And the other is the strangeness of Paul, his moodiness and "differentness," which lead Mrs. Morel to treat him specially and feel, deep in her heart, that he is somehow set apart from his brothers and sisters.

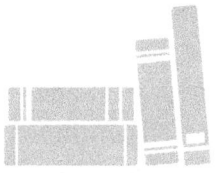

SONS AND LOVERS

TEXTUAL ANALYSIS

PART I: CHAPTERS 4 - 6

CHAPTER FOUR: THE YOUNG LIFE OF PAUL

Now Lawrence narrows the focus of the story even more; he is finally concentrating his attention on Paul, who is, after all, to be the protagonist of the novel. As a child, Paul is pale and quiet, "with eyes that seemed to listen. . . . As a rule, he seemed old for his years." He is extremely sensitive to other people's feelings, especially his mother's. When she frets, he understands, and can have no peace. Among the children, his earliest friend is his sister Annie, who is closest to him in age; the handsome William, whom he so much admires, is really too old for regular companionship. One day Paul accidentally breaks Annie's favorite doll, and a little while later he proposes that they "make a sacrifice of Arabella" by burning the doll on a makeshift altar. Annie is shocked and horrified by the mechanism of Paul's guilt, which makes him seem to hate the doll so intensely because he has broken it.

Like the other children - perhaps even more - Paul is quite hostile to his father. Morel continues to bully and drink as always, and one evening William comes home to find his mother with a black eye. While the other children cower in a corner, William and Morel come dangerously close to a fist fight. Mrs. Morel finally calms them down, but like all his other negative experiences with their father, this one leaves its mark on the sensitive Paul.

When William gets older, the family moves from The Bottoms to another house, on top of a hill which looks out over the whole valley through which the mines and towns are scattered. In front of the house is a huge old ash tree, which shrieks terrifyingly when the wind sweeps through it. Also, "having such a great space in front of them" gives the children a feeling "of night, of vastness, and of terror. This terror came in from the shrieking of the tree and the anguish of the home discord." Often, especially in their first winter in the new house, when Morel's drunkenness is very bad, Paul is wakened at night by the sound of his parents quarreling. "And then came the horror of the sudden silence, silence everywhere, outside and downstairs. What was it? Was it a silence of blood? What had he done?" Night after night, too, Morel is late for dinner, then comes home to wolf his food brutishly and fall into a drunken stupor in the kitchen.

And yet, Lawrence tells us, when he is sober and working around the house, the children, even Paul, enjoy being with their father. He is "a good workman, dexterous, and one who, when he was in a good humour, always sang." On such happy evenings, also, Morel likes to tell the children stories of his work in the pit, and then to go to bed early. After he's in bed everyone feels secure and they all "cuddle closely in the warmth."

As a child, Paul is delicate and subject to bronchitis. His mother doesn't fuss over him, but when he is sick he never wants to be separated from her. Though his father is often kind to him at such times, it is really only his mother he wants. Indeed, the boy is so devoted to his mother that when he is well and goes berry picking in the summer, he often will walk all day, "rather than own himself beaten and come home to her empty - handed."

One of Paul's most traumatic childhood occurrences is the weekly experience of going to pick up his father's salary in the mining company office. This job, which passes from one child to the next as each outgrows it, is one which Paul especially hates. He hates being jammed into the crowded waiting room, among a packed group of "common and hateful" men, who "always stan' in front of me, so's I can't get out." And even more, he hates being lectured and condescended to by the pompous clerk who doles out little sermons along with the pay.

On Fridays, Mrs. Morel goes marketing, and Paul stays home to do the baking. He loves to "stop in and draw or read," and then, later, to hear all about his mother's experiences at the little hilltop marketplace where she shops for lace and pottery as well as food. When she comes home with her treasures, the two exclaim over them together - a cheap little china dish, a handful of pansies, can charm and delight them both for days.

On winter evenings, when the weather is clear, the few children who live on Scargill Street - the hillside street where the Morels' new house is - romp in the circle of light around the single lamppost. They are "brought exceedingly close together, owing to their isolation" so that "if a quarrel took place, the whole play was spoiled." Nevertheless, "they all loved the Scargill Street house for its openness, for the great scallop of the world it had in view."

When William goes to London to work, the Morels are poorer than usual, for the young man has many expenses in the city and can't send his mother as much money as he'd given her before. The preparations for his Christmas visit are incredibly elaborate, though, for he is still the favorite, the "knight" of the family, out doing battle in the world for Mrs. Morel. When his train is two hours late, his mother frets and worries. At last he arrives, bringing lavish gifts - a gold - handled umbrella for Mrs. Morel, turkish delight and crystallized pineapple for his brothers and sister. Suddenly the house seems overflowing with luxury and love.

That summer William has a chance to go on a cheap cruise to the Mediterranean during his two week vacation. But instead he comes home, which, of course, "compensated his mother for much."

Comment

This chapter is another compendium of scenes of family life, most of them focusing on Paul, but some still dealing with Mr. and Mrs. Morel, William, Annie and Arthur. Increasingly, however, we are seeing events and characters from young Paul's point of view instead of through the eyes of his parents, as we did earlier.

The rather loose way in which the chapter is organized - skipping back and forth among various times and places - may at first seem confusing, but it contributes to the rich sense of reality that is being built up around the Morels. Not only do we see them in dramatic situations - family fights, partings, reunions and sicknesses - but we get to know the ordinary pattern and texture of their daily life, the games around the lamppost, the marketing and baking, the blackberrying, the financial problems, the minor illnesses and convalescences. After a while we begin to feel we know these people as well as we know our next door neighbors, or perhaps our nearest relatives. More important, all this contributes to an air of passing time, a long tunnel of years through which Paul must pass, that is an essential component of any bildungsroman, for the growth, the maturing, the ripening of a personality is more a product of years of repeated routine than of individual dramatic experiences. Thus, the scenes from the daily life of the Morels, which form the substance of this chapter, are more than background. In themselves they constitute an essential part of the action of the novel.

One other important point is the incident of Paul and the doll. As in the stories of Paul's bronchitis, his sensitivity and his intense dependence on his mother, this incident helps to underline the differentness of this son, that special quality of his which his mother noticed from the beginning and which gives her love for him a tinge of anguish and morbidity. It is this, this quality which will end up by making the boy into the artist he is to become, and this quality which makes him the hero of this particular bildungsroman.

CHAPTER FIVE: PAUL LAUNCHES INTO LIFE

When Paul is fourteen, Walter Morel, who is "rather a heedless man, careless of danger," and therefore has "endless accidents," is hurt in a typical mine mishap. A piece of rock falls on his leg, smashing it, and he has to be taken to the hospital in Nottingham, where his wife dutifully visits him twice a week. She is "grieved" by his pain, and "bitterly sorry" for him, but still, "in her heart of hearts, where the love should have burned, there was a blank." The children also feel sorry for their father, but they too appreciate the cheerfulness and tranquillity that pervade the house when he is away. Paul especially enjoys it. "I'm the man in the house now," he tells his mother "with joy."

The time has finally come for Paul to find a job. At fourteen he is considered old enough for full -time employment, and the Morel family badly needs whatever money he can make. He hates the idea of work; already he feels like "a prisoner of industrialism." As he sits in the library, looking through want ads, he feels that he is "being taken into bondage. His freedom in the beloved home valley was going now." William helps Paul to write a letter of application, and we are told that Paul's handsome older brother is becoming "quite swanky" in London. He never sends his mother money anymore; his friends are all "gentlemen" and he is seeing a good deal of a girl he met at a dance, a "tall and elegant" brunette, "after whom the men were running thick and fast." Mrs. Morel, of course, disapproves violently, fearing that the girl will trap her son in an unsuitable marriage.

Paul is soon called for an interview by one of the firms to which he has applied, and he and his mother go up to Nottingham together for the day. Thomas Jordan, Manufacturer of Surgical Appliances, is the owner of the small but prosperous factory which produces trusses, elastic bandages, artificial limbs, etc. Mr. Jordan himself is "a red - faced, white - whiskered" little man who tests Paul's French during the interview, complains about the boy's execrable handwriting and then hires him at eight shillings a week. He and his mother celebrate this dubious victory with an expensive restaurant dinner and some shopping. After "a perfect afternoon' they arrive home tired and happy.

In the meantime, William sends his mother a photograph of his girlfriend, Louisa Lily Denys Western, nicknamed "Gyp" or

"Gypsy." But Mrs. Morel thinks the picture, taken in a low - cut gown, quite improper.

Several days after his interview, Paul starts work as a clerk for Jordan. He must work a twelve hour day; to be in time he has to catch the 7:15 train for Nottingham each morning, and he doesn't get home again until after 9 at night. He hates the long hours and the grubbiness of the factory, but soon comes to like his immediate superior, Mr. Pappleworth, and most of the other employees. His special friends, however, are the factory girls who sew the trusses and other "surgical appliances." Polly, their foreman, heats his dinner for him at noon, and he is also fond of Fanny, a sensitive hunchback; Connie, a shy redhead; Louie, a bold flirtatious girl; and Emma, who is plain and rather old, but condescendingly kind. After a while, too, Paul comes to enjoy the train ride home at night. He likes "to watch the lights of the town, sprinkled thick on the hills, fusing together in a blaze in the valleys. He [feels] rich in life and happy." As soon as he gets home he tells all the little events of his day to Mrs. Morel. "His life - story, like an Arabian nights, was told night after night to his mother. It was almost as if it were her own life."

Comment

In this chapter Paul's world, which has been narrowly limited to his Family and the small mining town where he was born, expands to include the Jordan factory in the nearby city of Nottingham, as well as the city itself. And though the boy returns every night to his mother with the full "budget" of his day's experiences, we can see that his separation from her - the process of growth and breaking away from home which is one of the main **themes** of the novel - has already begun. Indeed, Paul himself, in his reluctance to leave his "beloved home valley" seems to sense the coming maturity which must inevitably cut him off from his mother, as well as from his birthplace. The scenes dealing with William and his girlfriend also foreshadow this future development in Paul, for William, several steps ahead of his brother, has already clashed with his mother over girls and jobs and money. Thus the main battle - lines of the novel are now already drawn: on the one side, the mother, passionately devoted to her sons, wanting to live for and through them; on the other, the sons, equally devoted to their mother, but anxious, too, like all healthy young growing things, to live for and through themselves. It is this conflict between these diametrically opposed needs of Mrs. Morel and her sons, especially her son Paul, which will be at the heart of the novel.

CHAPTER SIX: A DEATH IN THE FAMILY

As Arthur Morel grows up, he becomes increasingly difficult. A beautiful, intelligent boy, he nevertheless flies into frequent rages "over nothing" and often seems "unbearably raw and irritable." He especially dislikes his father, who has grown "mean and rather despicable" instead of ripening with the years. Thus when Arthur wins a scholarship to the Grammar School in Nottingham, his mother decides to let him live in town with her sister, coming home only on weekends. And with Annie working at the Board - School, Mrs. Morel clings more and more to Paul. He is "quiet and not brilliant," but everything this dutiful son does is for his mother. "The two shared lives."

William is now engaged to "his brunette" and at Christmas he brings her home to meet his parents. "Gypsy," as she is called, is a tall, handsome girl, with hardly a thought in her head that isn't about clothes and flirtations. At first she's quite uppity with the Morels, treating Annie and Paul as servants. Nevertheless, the children worship her for her beautiful outfits and her fine London manners. Mrs. Morel, however, is more than ever fearful that "Gyp" will ruin her son, and she tries hard to convince him to give the girl up. When William comes home alone at Easter, he even admits to his mother that "when I'm away from her I don't care for her a bit. . . . But then, when I'm with her in the evenings, I am awfully fond of her."

In the meantime, Paul is doing well at Jordan's. His wages have even been raised to ten shillings weekly. But his health suffers "from the long hours and the confinement." One afternoon when he's on holiday from work, his mother decides to take him, for a treat, up to Willey Farm, where her friends Mr. and Mrs. Leivers have just moved with their children. Both Paul and Mrs. Morel are enchanted by the country. The farm is full of wonderful flowers and woods, which they delightedly admire. Mrs. Leivers herself is invalided, but she is glad to see her visitors and introduces them to her fourteen - year - old daughter Miriam, a shy, sensitive girl who loves poetry and tends to be frightened of animals and athletics. Her brothers, Geoffrey and Maurice, twelve and thirteen, tease her about her fears. "Durstn't jump off a gate, durstn't tweedle, durstn't go on a slide, durstn't stop a girl hittin' her. She can do nowt but go about thinkin' herself somebody. 'The Lady of the Lake!' Yah!" cries Maurice. But Paul tries to make friends with the shy girl anyway. He and his mother also meet Mr. Leivers, the children's father, and Edgar, eighteen, the oldest boy. When they leave, they feel they have spent a memorable day.

In the late spring William and "Gyp" came home again. All the Morels can see that there is a terrible conflict going on in William. His fiancee is so shallow, so empty headed and foolish that one part of him despises her, though another part of him is still powerfully drawn by her beauty. In his eyes as he looks at her, is "a certain baffled look of misery and fierce appreciation." Throughout the summer, William's letters have "a feverish tone; he seemed unnatural and intense. Sometimes he was exaggeratedly jolly, usually he was flat and bitter. . . . 'Ay,' his mother said, 'I'm afraid he's ruining himself against that creature, who isn't worthy of his love - no, no more than a rag doll.'" Then, one day in October, shortly after the young man has been home for a two day visit, the Morels get a telegram. William is ill in London with pneumonia. Mrs. Morel rushes to his side, but within eight hours he is dead.

Mr. Morel goes up to London to help his wife. He is "scared and peaked," and the children are numb with shock as William's body is brought home for burial. In some of his most moving prose Lawrence describes the homecoming of the coffin.

There was the noise of wheels. Outside in the darkness of the street below Paul could see horses and a black vehicle, one lamp, and a few pale faces; then some men, miners, all in their shirt - sleeves, seemed to struggle in the obscurity. Presently two men appeared, bowed beneath a great weight. It was Morel and his neighbour.

"Steady!" called Morel out of breath. He and his fellow mounted the steep garden step, heaved into the candle - light with their gleaming coffin - end. Limbs of other men were seen struggling behind. Morel and Burns, in front, staggered; the great dark weight swayed.

"Steady, steady!" cried Morel, as if in pain. . . . The coffin swayed, the men began to mount the three steps with their load. Annie's candle flickered, and she whimpered as the first men appeared, and the limbs and bowed heads of six men struggled to climb into the room, bearing the coffin that rode like sorrow on their living flesh.

"Oh, my son - my son!" Mrs. Morel sang softly, and each time the coffin swung to the unequal climbing of the men: "Oh my son - my son - my son!"

After William's death Mrs. Morel is paralyzed with grief. She cannot be persuaded to take "her old bright interest in life," no matter how Paul tries. The boy, for his part, feels desolate and deserted by his mother, who can only "brood on her dead son." Finally, however, Paul becomes dangerously ill with pneumonia and almost dies himself. Thus Mrs. Morel is finally roused from her trance of despair, and her life now roots itself in Paul.

As William had once predicted, within three months of his death Lily ("Gypsy") is enjoying herself at balls and parties. But the Morels are "gentle with each other for some time after the death of their son."

Comment

A number of important things happen in this chapter. First of all, the whole story of William - who briefly becomes the center of attention once more - has important repercussions for Paul's life throughout the rest of the book. The relationship between William and Lily, like the relationship between the Morels, is one of struggle and conflict. But in this case the main conflict is internal: it is William's struggle with himself, the battle between his sexual attraction to Lily and his intellectual contempt for her. There is also the important struggle between William and his mother over his relationship with Lily - a conflict which prefigures similar situations between Paul and Mrs. Morel. The important thing to note is that here, as almost everywhere in Lawrence's writing, the relationship of a man and a woman is fraught with tension and conflict.

William's death is also obviously a family event of the greatest magnitude. Not only does it bring the children their first meaningful contact with death and grief, but perhaps more significant, it elevates Paul to the important position, previously held by William, of eldest son. No matter how close Paul and his mother had been before, while William was alive William was Mrs. Morel's first love. Now, however, no one comes between her and Paul, and her life roots itself in the being of her second son.

Another significant event in this chapter is Paul's and his mother's visit to the Leivers' farm. Willey Farm and its inhabitants are to become increasingly important in the boy's life, as we shall see in the next chapter, and Miriam Leivers is to become perhaps most important of all. Indeed, along with Paul and Mrs. Morel, Miriam is one of the three central characters of *Sons and Lovers*, and it is over his relationship with her that Paul's great battle with his mother - and himself - will have to be waged.

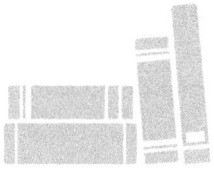

SONS AND LOVERS

TEXTUAL ANALYSIS

PART II: CHAPTERS 7 - 11

CHAPTER SEVEN: LAD AND GIRL LOVE

This long and detailed chapter is almost exclusively concerned, as its title indicates, with the development of the relationship between Paul and Miriam. Miriam, as we have learned earlier, is a shy, sensitive, romantic girl, who loves poetry and the novels of Walter Scott and resents being kept at home to do housework. Her beauty is "that of a shy, wild, quiveringly sensitive thing," but she has rather little self -esteem, fearing that people will think of her as a "swine - girl" and not see "the princess" underneath. She worships Paul for his quickness and creativity and learning. Paul, for his part, spends a good deal of time at the Leivers farm in the ten months that he is out of work convalescing from his bout of pneumonia. As time passes, he comes to be closest to Mrs. Leivers, the warm, sympathetic, religiously - inclined mother of the family; Edgar, the rational, intelligent, practical, oldest son; and Miriam.

Miriam and Paul go regularly to the library together every Thursday night. They share most of their intellectual experiences, and Miriam encourages Paul to show her the paintings and sketches he is constantly working on. Her intensity warms - and sometimes repels - him. Her attitude toward her younger brother, five-year-old Hubert, especially annoys him. She often clasps the child "in an ecstasy of love" and at such times Paul wishes she would be more "ordinary." But Miriam can never be ordinary. "All the life of Miriam's body," Lawrence tells us, "was in her eyes, which were usually dark as a dark church, but could flame with light like a conflagration. Her face scarcely ever altered from its look of brooding. . . . There was no looseness or abandon about her. Everything was gripped stiff with intensity, and her effort, overcharged, closed in on itself."

One day when Miriam is complaining that she has been denied an education because she is a girl, Paul offers to teach her algebra. At first the girl is reluctant, but finally she agrees to try to learn from him. But she is not quick at it, and she tends, as in everything, to become overemotional when she fails. This enrages Paul, and he often has terrible fits of anger at her. She never reproaches him for this, and he is often "cruelly ashamed." When he sees "her hand trembling and her mouth parted with suffering," his heart is "scalded with pain for her." And because of the intensity to which she rouses him, he seeks her.

Mrs. Morel, of course, dislikes Miriam. Whenever Paul is out late with the girl, he knows his mother is "fretting and getting angry about him - why, he [can] not understand." But Mrs. Morel thinks Miriam is "one of those who will want to suck a man's soul out til he has none left. . . . She will never let him become a man; she never will." She accuses him of "courting" Miriam and "it is disgusting - bits of lads and girls courting." But Paul thinks his relationship with Miriam is purely abstract and Platonic. "That there was any love growing between him and Miriam, neither of them would have acknowledged. He thought he was too sane for such sentimentality, and she thought herself too lofty. They both were late in coming to maturity, and psychical ripeness was much beyond even the physical. Miriam was exceedingly sensitive, as her mother had always been. The slightest grossness made her recoil almost in anguish. . . . Paul took his pitch from her, and their intimacy went on in an utterly chaste fashion. It could never be mentioned that the mare was in foal."

When Paul is nineteen, he is only earning twenty shillings a week, but he is happy enough. His painting is going well and life is good. He and Miriam go on several excursions with friends during the Easter holiday, visiting points of interest near Nottingham. On their way home from one trip, Miriam sees Paul standing in the road, trying to fix his umbrella. Something about the way the light is hitting him is mysteriously moving and painful to her. "Quivering as at some 'annunciation,'" she realizes that she is in love with him. Later she learns that the umbrella had belonged to his dead brother William, and that he was taking so much trouble over it for his mother's sake. After this strange incident there is a kind of sexual tension between Paul and Miriam which becomes increasingly insistent. Just before one of his visits, the girl even prays - "O Lord, let me not love Paul Morel. Keep me from loving him, if I ought not love him. . . . But . . . if it is Thy will that I should love him, make me love him - as Christ would, who died for the souls of men. Make me love him splendidly, because he is Thy son."

That summer Miriam and the Morels, alone with some other young friends of the children's, go for a two week holiday to the seashore. One night, as Paul and Miriam are walking along the beach, they stop to look at the full moon, which is rising enormous and orange over the dunes. Miriam is "deeply moved and religious," but Paul feels his heart beating "heavily, the muscles of his arms contracted.... 'What is it'" Miriam asks. His blood is "concentrated like a flame in his chest." But he cannot get his problem across to her, for he hardly knows himself what is wrong. The fact, as Lawrence puts it, "that he might want her as a man wants a woman had in him been suppressed into a shame." Their "purity" is preventing "even their first love - kiss." And with all these strains and tensions between them, it is no wonder that even while he loves her, Paul also hates Miriam, feeling that she somehow spoils "his ease and naturalness."

Comment

Just as the relationship of the Morels was marred by conflict and torment, just as William had struggled to master his feelings for Lily, so the relationship of Paul and Miriam is fraught with conflict. But since Miriam is almost the exact opposite of Lily, her faults are the opposite of Lily's. Where the relationship of William and Lily was based almost entirely on sexual attraction, without any spiritual communion, Paul and Miriam have only a spiritual relationship. Their main struggle, we can see, will be about sex. But in any case - as always in Lawrence - love involves a struggle, whether a struggle for understanding, for contact, for mastery, or for communication.

Of course, as there was with William, there is also a conflict between Paul and his mother over Miriam, for though the girl has become increasingly important in his life, Mrs. Morel is still her son's chief confidante and counselor, his first and greatest love. Indeed, perhaps it is because of his devotion to his mother that the boy, during his earliest visits to Willey Farm, first turns to Mrs. Leivers, rather than Miriam, for understanding and friendship. His primary impulse is always to seek out the mother - figure, because of his deep feeling for his own mother. Only when his young manhood begins to assert itself does he find himself increasingly drawn to the daughter, though without knowing why.

As we have noted earlier, much of *Sons and Lovers* is a very accurate and conscious record of D. H. Lawrence's own early life. Indeed when the author came to write these sections dealing with Willey Farm and the Leivers, especially Miriam, he called on Jessie Chambers, the original of Miriam, to verify the truth of his recollections. As a matter of fact, at some points Jessie went a step beyond mere criticism. She actually set down her own memories in a narrative which Lawrence simply rewrote and included in the book. The incident of the umbrella, which is told with such intensity from Miriam's point of view, is a good example. Jessie recalled and recorded the incident; Lawrence rewrote and refined her report. Thus in a few places *Sons and Lovers* was actually a collaboration between Lawrence and Jessie Chambers. (Lawrence, as is obvious, was a good collaborator, at least when it came to rewriting other people's work. *The Boy in the Bush*, a later book of his, was originally a novel written by a nurse whom Lawrence met in Australia. She sent it to him for criticism and he became enthusiastic enough to rewrite it. It has also been suggested that some translations from the Russian, published over the signature of S. S. Koteliansky, a friend of Lawrence's, were actually revised by the author at a time when he needed money.)

CHAPTER EIGHT: STRIFE IN LOVE

One day Arthur, who still tends to be "wild and restless," always getting into all kinds of scrapes, runs off to the nearby town of Derby with a friend and enlists in the army. His mother tries to get him out but can't, and his father, furious at this piece of foolishness, claims he will disown him. In comparison to his younger brother, Paul is a model son. He even wins two first prizes for his paintings at a show in Nottingham. His mother is full of pride in him. She is confident that he will distinguish himself in the world, and now her life is "rich with promise."

One afternoon as Paul is walking in Nottingham he meets Miriam with a friend of hers, Clara Dawes. Clara is a haughty, sensual - looking blonde who is separated from her husband and has taken up Women's Rights. She is "supposed to be clever," which of course interests Paul. Baxter Dawes, her husband, works in Paul's factory - where Clara herself had once worked also - , but he is an unpleasant bully who has taken an intense dislike to Morel from the first day he met him.

Later Miriam questions Paul about his reaction to Clara. We learn that she has cultivated this woman mainly because of her (Clara's) connection with Paul's work: Miriam wants to find out more about Paul's Nottingham environment. But it almost seems as though she is painfully aware of the way in which Clara's air of sensuality contrasts with her own spiritual aura. Paul too finds Miriam's spirituality painful. Sometimes he is "mad to comfort her and kiss her. But then he dared not or could not. There was something prevented him. His kisses were wrong for her."

At home Mrs. Morel is increasingly hostile to Miriam. When Miriam and her brother Edgar come to tea, Paul's mother is kind to the young man but barely civil to the girl. She complains, as always, that Miriam wants to "absorb" her lover. And Paul, coming home from his walks with Miriam, is also "wild with torture." Why must he be so torn? he wonders. "Why did his mother sit at home and suffer? . . . And why did he hate Miriam, and feel so cruel towards her, at the thought of his mother?"

On Friday nights Miriam often comes down to the Morel's house for a French lesson from Paul. But before she comes, Walter Morel and his pit - buddies share out their wages. On one particular Friday, Mrs. Morel goes off for her marketing cross because her husband has only left her twenty - five shillings from his salary. Paul, who is staying behind to mind the baking and wait for Miriam, tells her that "you can have my money. Let him go to hell." Later, when Miriam comes, he shows her a textile design he has done - all "wonderful reddish roses and dark green stems, all so simple and somehow so wicked - looking." Then he begins to talk about the design. For him there is "the most intense pleasure in talking about his work to Miriam. . . . She brought forth to him his imaginations."

While Paul and Miriam are talking, Annie's friend Beatrice, a bold young student - teacher, arrives. She totally destroys their mood by flirting so wildly with Paul that he lets the bread burn in the oven. Miriam is left desolate, as usual, and Paul, when Bea leaves, feels guilty, and cruel. Later that night, after taking Miriam home, he tries to apologize to his mother, who is sitting white - faced by the fire, looking reproachful. But it seems that Mrs. Morel is actually ill, perhaps suffering from heart - trouble. Walter Morel comes home drunk to find Paul kissing and comforting his mother and declaring that he will give up Miriam. "I've never - you know, Paul - I've never had a husband - not really - " Mrs. Morel whimpers. "At your mischief again?" sneers Morel, "venomously" from the doorway." Within a minute Paul and his father have almost come to blows when the mother gives a little moan and seems to faint in her chair. As Paul helps his mother up the stairs to bed, he implores her to "sleep with Annie, mother, not with him. . . . Don't sleep with him, mother." Later in his own bed he presses his face upon the pillow "in a fury of misery. And yet, somewhere in his soul, he was at peace because he still loved his mother best."

Comment

In this chapter the relationship between Paul and his mother grows frankly Oedipal as Mrs. Morel's hostility to Miriam becomes more and more irrepressible. It is interesting to note that the Friday night which ends with Paul almost openly making love to his mother begins with a scene in which Gertrude Morel washes her husband's back while Paul rather enviously admires his father's youthfully handsome body. And that evening - so fraught with sexual tension and significance - also includes, we should notice, the scene of wild flirtation with Beatrice and the scene of "spiritual intercourse" between Paul and Miriam, as well as some moments in which Paul is sexually tempted by Miriam, then put off by her spirituality. Later it seems as though Paul is pouring all of the passion and devotion which he might have had for this girl into his care for his mother. And his mother, for her part, honestly admits that Paul must take the place of the husband she feels she never "really" had.

Women like Gertrude Morel are quite common. Everyone has seen cases of mothers who don't want to "let their sons go," who insist on living through them and never give the boys a chance to become real men in their relationships with other women. But in *Sons and Lovers* Lawrence seems to have captured the essence of such a woman, and of such mother - son involvements in a series of powerfully passionate scenes, Lawrence, who had this kind of attachment to his own mother, came to feel, as he got older, that such a relationship was a perversion of a woman's natural love for her child, that such a woman, with her pseudo - sexual teasing, aroused an unfulfillable, hopeless sexual passion in her son which ended up by turning the boy in on himself and making him an "introvert." (Cf. *Fantasia of the Unconscious*) And certainly Paul becomes increasingly tormented and torn by inner struggles as the action of *Sons and Lovers* progresses. But, as we shall see, time, chance, and the young man's own talents eventually combine to bring him out of this early agony relatively whole and unscarred.

CHAPTER NINE: DEFEAT OF MIRIAM

As time goes by, the "battle" between Paul and Miriam becomes more intense. By spring he has "a good deal against her," and she is vaguely aware of it. She believes that she must eventually "sacrifice" herself to her love for Paul. Certainly she never imagines herself "living happily through a lifetime with him." One day when he comes to see her during the Easter holidays he is restless and disagreeable. When she takes him out to see some new - blown daffodils in her backyard he is irritated by her romantic intensity. Later in the afternoon he tells her that he thinks they'd "better break off" their relationship because he can never love her. But Miriam senses Gertrude Morel's influence behind both his words and his mood.

Indeed, Lawrence tell us, Paul has "come back to his mother. Hers [is] the strongest tie in his life" . . . it is the one place in the world that stands solid and does not "melt into unreality." And for Mrs. Morel the same thing is true; her life centers on Paul's just as Paul's pivots around hers. Because of this she can't tolerate his relationship with Miriam. She is fighting "to keep Paul." Yet despite the strength of his attachment to his mother, the boy's "new young life, so strong and imperious, was urged towards something else." Mrs. Morel sees this and wishes that Miriam were "a woman who could take this new life of his, and leave her the roots." But Paul's problem is that both women - Gertrude and Miriam - want to devour him utterly.

Paul continues to see Miriam, though he periodically threatens to cut off their friendship completely. During this period, however, he does spend more time than before with Edgar, for he is so passionately attached to Willey Farm and the entire Leivers Family that, hostile as he is to Miriam, he can never leave off coming to the farm to see somebody. But Miriam broods over his split with her. She feels sure that underneath all the conscious turmoil of his mind Paul still loves and needs her as much as ever. Nevertheless, she decides that his chief need in life is "herself." If she can "prove it, both to herself and to him, the rest might go; she could simply trust to the future."

To "prove" Paul's faithfulness, Miriam invites Clara Dawes to spend a day at Willey Farm. She senses that Paul is sexually interested in this attractive, slightly older woman, and she wants to demonstrate that his "higher" desires (for herself) will conquer his "lower" desires (for Clara). She forgets, says Lawrence, that her terms of "higher" and "lower" are "arbitrary."

The day with Clara proves inconclusive. Paul is still attracted to her, excited and teasing in her presence. For her part, Clara is hostile to him at first; she is determinedly feminist and scorns his flirtations. But by the end of the afternoon Paul has realized that there is more to Clara than he thought. She is deeply unhappy and he wonders why. "He could tell by the way she moved, as if she didn't care, that she suffered."

One day Paul takes his mother to Lincoln to see the Cathedral, and when she can hardly climb a hill to sightsee he is furious with pain and despair. "Why can't a man have a young mother?" he exclaims. "What is she old for?" Later they talk about Clara - and Mrs. Morel objects that she's too old (thirty) for Paul, who is twenty - three. But she is not "hostile to the idea of Clara" as she is to Miriam.

In the meantime a number of things seem to be changing in the Morel family. Annie is getting married and Arthur, who has turned out handsome and restless, is home on leave from the army. Since he is so discontented, Mrs. Morel decides to buy him out of the service, and now he acts "like a lad taking a holiday," he is so joyful and relieved. During his furlough he scorns his flirtations. But by the end of the afternoon Paul has flirts madly with Beatrice Wyld (the same Beatrice who flirted "life changing around him." At last all this restlessness and change drives him away from Miriam and into a closer relationship with Clara. Finally he even writes a rather cruel letter to Miriam - "You see," he tells her, "I can give you a spirit love, I have given it you this long, long time; but not embodied passion. See, you are a nun. I have given you what I would give a holy nun - as a mystic monk to a mystic nun. Surely you esteem it best." The first phase of their love - affair is over, for though Paul is still a virgin, his sex - instinct has now become too strong for Miriam and he is slowly turning toward Clara Dawes, hoping to find in her the passionate response which Miriam has refined out of her own life.

Comment

Lawrence focuses on a comparatively new conflict in this chapter, although the conflicts between Miriam and Gertrude Morel (for possession of Paul) and between Paul and Gertrude Morel (for Paul's freedom) also continue to be central. But a good deal more attention is given to the polarity between conventional sexual purity (based on a kind of religious idealism) and liberated sexual response, a polarity on which the "new" struggle between Miriam and Clara, another struggle for Paul's love, will be based. In a sense, this battle of emotions and beliefs - which Miriam would call a battle between "higher" and "lower," too - is also raging within Paul. So far he has allowed

Miriam's "purity" to refine his own sexuality out of existence. Rather than turn to other women he has, as it were, sublimated this instinct by channeling all his unfulfilled passions into his artistic pursuits, his passionate devotion to his mother and his increasing hostility to Miriam. But now his awakening sexual urges can no longer be denied. When Miriam - to "prove" his love - brings him together with Clara, she half - consciously prepares the way for the emotional crisis that must soon come to Paul.

CHAPTER TEN: CLARA

When he is twenty - three, Paul wins first prize in an art show at Nottingham, and his painting is bought for twenty guineas by a prominent local citizen. His mother is overjoyed. "Hurrah, my boy!" she cries, in a triumphant frenzy. "I knew we should do it!" Soon the news has spread all over town, and people look at Paul with new respect. Even his father is impressed, and Mr. Jordan, his employer, actually invites him to dinner. It seems as though a new life is starting for Paul. New social vistas open up before him, and his mother begins to dream that he will make a good marriage some day. But Paul tells her that "I don't want to belong to the well - to - do middle class. I like my common people best. I belong to the common people."

Almost imperceptibly Paul is drifting away from Miriam. Though he is unaware of the change himself, he is slowly giving more and more of himself to his relationship with Clara. It all seems to start when he visits her house to bring her a message one day. He meets her mother, a large, stout woman with severe features, who yet seems to have "the strength and sang-froid of a woman in the prime of life." She and Clara, who no longer works at Jordan's, are reduced to spinning lace at home for a living - "sweated" work, as almost all women's work was at that time.

When he sees her in these surroundings, Paul begins to realize that the proud Clara may not be so cold and independent as she seems. He experiences "a thrill of joy, thinking she might need his help. She seemed denied and deprived of so much. And her arm moved mechanically that should never have been subdued to a mechanism, and her head was bowed to the lace, that never should have been bowed. She seemed to be stranded there among the refuse that life has thrown away, doing her jennying."

Paul helps Clara to get her old job at Jordan's back, and now that she is working there again, he sees her every day, and their relationship slowly blossoms, becoming more intricate and intense as time goes by. The other girls, Clara's underlings (she is the foreman), dislike Clara; her natural coolness and reserve keep her from making friends with them. Furthermore, Clara, intelligent and painfully self-educated, feels herself "above" factory work. But all this combines to drive her closer to Paul. When the other girls chip in to buy Paul an expensive set of paints as a birthday present, they deliberately exclude Clara. Paul takes her for a walk to console her and then, later, she sends him a book of poetry, which he knows she can't afford. Finally they are close enough to discuss Clara's marriage to Baxter Dawes. She tells Paul that she was married at twenty-two, but that Dawes "never really mattered to me.... I seemed to have been asleep nearly all my life." In the end, she says, she left Dawes because "He wanted to bully me because he hadn't got me. And then I felt as if I wanted to run, as if I was fastened and bound up."

As their relationship intensifies, Paul is more and more attracted to Clara. And yet, because she is still a married woman, he believes that theirs is only a "simple friendship.... He was like so many young men of his own age," Lawrence explains. "Sex had become so complicated in him that he would have denied that he ever could want Clara or Miriam or any woman whom he knew.

Sex desire was a sort of detached thing, that did not belong to a woman." And when he and Clara (whose own friendship with Miriam has weakened considerably of late, for obvious reasons) discuss Miriam one day, Clara astonishes him by asserting that Miriam "doesn't want any of your soul communion. That's your own imagination. She wants you." "But she seems . . ." he begins. "You've never tried," Clara interrupts.

Comment

In this chapter we see more of the theoretical Lawrence than we have before. Lawrence hated industrialism, a feeling which was more or less inevitable, given his early experience with the worst aspects of nineteenth and twentieth century "progress" - the dim, grubby coal - mining towns of the English Midlands, where so much of nature has been permanently scarred and despoiled by man's soot and sweat. Thus there hangs over *Sons and Lovers* constantly, as over a good deal of Lawrence's work, the threatening black cloud that the Industrial Revolution has cast over all of modern society. Clara, that proud and splendid animal, is only an example of the way in which Lawrence thinks a beautiful body can be painfully bent to mechanism. Baxter Dawes, as we shall see later, and Paul's own father, Walter Morel, as we have already seen, are also good examples of the way in which Lawrence believes industrialism can warp and pervert naturally healthy organisms. Thus no matter how hostile he is to Miriam, Paul is perpetually drawn to Willey Farm. There, he feels, as Lawrence himself always did, man is in harmony with nature; on the land a man lives by natural rhythms of birth, growth, death and renewal, and therefore he is freer to flourish himself, with his natural urges relatively undistorted. In a famous passage in *The Rainbow* Lawrence described this kind of farm life:

The Brangwens had lived for generations on the Marsh Farm, in the meadows where the Erewash twisted sluggishly through alder trees, separating Derbyshire from Nottinghamshire. . . . They felt the rush of the sap in spring, they knew the wave which cannot halt, but every year throws forward the seed to begetting, and, falling back, leaves the young - born on the earth. They knew the intercourse between heaven and earth, sunshine drawn into the breast and bowels, the rain sucked up in the daytime, nakedness that comes under the wind in autumn, showing the birds' nests no longer worth hiding. Their life and interrelations were such; feeling the pulse and body of the soil, that opened to their furrow for the grain, and became smooth and supple after their ploughing, and clung to their feet with a weight that pulled like desire, lying hard and unresponsive when the crops were to be shorn away. The young corn waved and was silken, and the lustre slid along the limbs of the men who saw it. They took the udder of the cows, the cows' yielded milk and pulse against the hands of the men, the pulse of the blood of the teats of the cows beat into the pulse of the hands of the men. They mounted their horses, and held life between the grip of their knees, they harnessed their horses at the wagon, and, with hand on the bridle - rings, drew the heaving of the horses after their will. . . . So much warmth and generating and pain and death did they know in their blood, earth and sky and beast and green plants, so much exchange and interchange they had with these, that they lived full and surcharged, their senses full fed, their faces always turned to the heat of the blood, staring into the sun, dazed with looking towards the source of generation, unable to turn round.

Of course, Lawrence did not imagine that farming, in particular, was any kind of panacea for human ills. For one thing, he recognized that farm life was, after all, only one step removed from town life. Willey Farm was outside Nottingham but not on another planet. The evils of industrialism, as well as man's classic, perpetual faults, must reach and entangle the Leiverses as well as the Morels and the Daweses. Miriam's "purity," for example, her lack - or perhaps denial would be a better word - of sexuality, is as serious a moral ailment as industrialism in Lawrence's view, and it is to the examination and diagnosis of this ill that he will devote himself in the next chapter.

CHAPTER ELEVEN: THE TEST ON MIRIAM

Clara's suggestion - that Miriam might actually want Paul as much as Paul wants her - brings the relationship between him and Miriam to a crisis. As always, Paul feels a return of his old inner conflict in the spring: he can't break off with Miriam, and yet he can't bring himself to approach her physically. "He would have given his head to have felt a joyous desire to marry her and to have her," Lawrence tells us, but there is some obstacle between them. Perhaps "the recoil and the shrinking from her" is "love in its first fierce modesty," Paul speculates, "a strong desire battling with a still stronger shyness and virginity." It seems "as if virginity were a positive force, which fought and won in both of them." Of course, in the midst of all this Mrs. Morel feels cast - off and left - out. Paul seems to be giving all his youth and energy to Miriam again, with nothing remaining for his mother. She keeps house for him mechanically, but the warmth is gone, at least temporarily, from their mutual devotion.

One night Paul states his problem frankly to Miriam. "Don't you think we have been too fierce in our what they call purity? Don't you think that to be so much afraid and averse is a sort of dirtiness?" Miriam is startled but finally forced to agree. Yet when Paul tries to kiss her he feels that "it hurt to do so." He feels he is "putting himself aside . . . sacrificed to her purity, which felt more like nullity." Yet, haltingly, their love - making advances. Before he leaves, as they walk outside in the dark, Paul kisses Miriam passionately. "In the darkness, where he could not see her, but only feel her, his passion flooded him. . . . 'Sometime you will have me?'" he asks. "'Not now,'" she replies. And "his hopes and his heart sank. A dreariness came over him." But after a minute "Miriam gripped her arms around him, and clenched her body stiff. 'You shall have me,' she said, through shut teeth."

Paul now courts Miriam like a lover. Yet the barriers between them remain. Too often, it seems to him, when he grows hot with passion, Miriam puts his face from her, and holds it between her hands looking tender and earnest. She can never relax and let him leave himself "to the great hunger and impersonality of passion; he must be brought back to a deliberate, reflective creature. As if from a swoon of passion she called him back to the littleness, the personal relationship."

About this time Miriam's grandmother becomes ill, and the girl is sent to keep house for her. Then, after a while, the grandmother leaves for a few days, and Miriam stays alone in the cottage to take care of things. When Paul comes to visit, it is more or less inevitable that they live together like husband and wife for a few days. But though Paul is dazzled by Miriam's beautiful body, their sexual relationship is not a success. The young man senses that the girl is sacrificing herself to his desire; she lies on the bed "like a creature awaiting immolation." When they discuss it, she begins to tremble. "You see - as we are - how can I get used to you?" she asks. "It would come all right if we were married." "You are always clenched against me," he complains. Agitated, she explains that "I'm not used to the thought . . . all my life mother said to me, 'there is one thing in marriage that is always dreadful, but you have to bear it.'" And

Paul sees that, sexually, things will never be natural and easy between him and Miriam.

After "a week of love" Paul tells his mother that he will see Miriam less. He begins to spend time with Clara again, and with men - friends that he has made in Nottingham. Finally he decides to break off with Miriam completely. On a Sunday in late summer he goes up to the farm early in the afternoon. Later, as he and Miriam are sitting by a stream, he tells her of his decision. "It's no good going on," he explains, "I don't want to marry. I don't want ever to marry. And if we're not going to marry, it's no good going on." When she protests that only a few days before he had wanted to marry her and she had refused him, he admits the unreasonableness of his feelings but insists that they are irrevocable this time. At last their relationship ends in a volley of mutual recriminations, with Miriam bitterly declaring that she had always known it would come to this and Paul furious at the idea that she had never been satisfied by their love. But as she goes home alone, in the new dress she had put on just for him, he stands still "with shame and pain in the highroad, thinking of the suffering he caused her." On his own way home he stops in a pub for a drink and flirts with "four hussies" he meets there, as if to forget his troubles. Yet when his mother looks at him that night she thinks that his gaiety seems "unreal. At the back of it [is] too much horror and misery."

Comment

This chapter focuses on crucial **episodes** between Paul and Miriam which contain the seeds of many of D. H. Lawrence's famous and controversial ideas about sex. Miriam's failure to respond to Paul sexually, as we have noted earlier, represents a serious moral flaw in her personality, a flaw which inevitably destroys what love Paul had for her. For as Paul - and Lawrence - sees it, she is denying the life in herself, the impersonal sexual urge which should transcend the "littleness" of the personal relationship. Lawrence, despite the notoriety of his philosophy on this subject, was hardly a garden - variety hedonist who advocated surrendering oneself entirely to promiscuous sexual pleasure. In fact, he was not a hedonist at all, but a true puritan, whose very mystical interpretation of man's sexual urge led him to condemn anyone who took sex lightly.

Thus, on the one hand, Lawrence would condemn the Don Juan type, who treats sex as a game, a sport, a pastime, to be indulged in with any woman who catches his eye, for such a man is violating the sacredness of the sex experience, which should be a kind of mystical union between one man and one woman who are, as it were, physically (and therefore spiritually) destined for one another. And, on the other hand, Lawrence would condemn the over - refined, virginal Miriam type, who treats sex as a "lower" expression of the "higher" spiritual feeling she has for her beloved, for such a woman misunderstands - and sentimentalizes - the relationship between lovers, a relationship in which the impersonal sexual expression of love is as high as - or higher than - the surface intimacy of "intellectual" and "spiritual" companionship.

Basically, sex, for Lawrence, is the one way in which a man and woman can in joining their bodies together, partake of, as it were, the universal life - energy. Thus the individual union - the "little" personal relationship - in sexual intercourse between a man and woman who are really suited to each other becomes part of a larger experience of the pulsing, tumultuous life - urge of the world, the great universal striving of the cosmos for life and yet more life. All this is very romantic, of course, and it is easy to see that Lawrence was not only writing in the nature -

oriented spirit of the Georgian poets, which was in turn based on the English tradition of Keats and Wordsworth, but also that his ideas reflect the more mystical romanticism of Germans like Goethe, Schiller and Nietzsche, who saw striving, change and tumult as the essence of life, and therefore as essential to the health of heroic man.

Actually, *Sons and Lovers* does not deal with these ideas as intensively as later works like *The Rainbow, Women in Love, The Plumed Serpent* and *Lady Chatterley's Lover*. But even here, for Paul to find himself as a man, he must come to terms with himself as a sexual being, a fact which he has begun increasingly to realize, and which has at last led to the collapse of his relationship with Miriam.

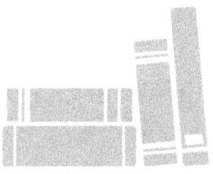

SONS AND LOVERS

TEXTUAL ANALYSIS

PART II: CHAPTERS 12 - 15

CHAPTER TWELVE: PASSION

Now that he has broken off with Miriam, Paul begins to see more of Clara and the more he sees her, the more passionately in love with her he falls, for Clara is everything that Miriam was not - a maturely sexual, ripely responsive woman. The two have a number of memorable meetings, which are described in some of Lawrence's most intensely lyrical passages. The first real change in their relationship occurs when they spend an afternoon walking along the banks of the river Trent, in the countryside outside Nottingham. There, as the river slides by "in a body, utterly silent and swift, intertwining among itself like some subtle, complex creature" their bodies are "sealed and annealed" in a first, passionate kiss. Later, on a secluded shore of the river, Clara gives herself to Paul, and afterwards, when she has misgivings, he consoles her lovingly, speaking (significantly) in his father's dialect. "But tha shouldna worrit," he murmurs softly, pleading.

Paul is now madly in love with Clara, and he invites her home to tea, to meet his mother. But in the meantime he is still seeing Miriam, whom he cannot entirely give up, for she continues to be one of his favorite intellectual companions. As Mrs. Morel puts it, "his and Miriam's affair [is] like a fire fed on books." Paul and Miriam discuss Clara, of course, and Paul explains to Miriam that Clara's marriage to Baxter Dawes had failed because she was only "half alive." "It was something like your father and mother," Miriam comments." "Yes; but my mother, I believe, got real joy and satisfaction out of my father at first," Paul replies. "I believe she had a passion for him; that's why she stayed with him." Then he adds that "That's what one must have . . . the real, real flame of feeling through another person - once, only once, if it only lasts three months. See, my mother looks as if she had everything that was necessary for her living and developing. There's not a tiny bit of a feeling of sterility about her." Miriam sees that Paul is seeking "a sort of baptism of fire in passion" and that he will never be satisfied until he has it. Well, then, she decides, she will let him "sow his wild oats," for she is still rather confident that he will eventually come back to her.

When Clara comes to tea at Paul's house, she and his mother get on rather well. Indeed, the whole afternoon goes off splendidly. Even Walter Morel is surprisingly gallant, and Clara finds the household almost frighteningly smooth, cool and competently run. The only hitch in the occasion occurs when Miriam stops in to say hello to her (by now) former friend, Clara. The two dislike each other intensely now, but Paul rather resents the way in which his mother and Clara seem to side together against Miriam. Later, when he sees Miriam leaving the chapel alone as he is leaving with Clara, after Sunday afternoon services, his heart is stung with remorse - which only, however, turns him more against her. Clara cannot, of course, help commenting on his obvious involvement. Paul tells her that he hopes always to be friends with Miriam, at which Clara coolly draws away from him. When he asks her what is wrong, she mockingly replies "You'd better run after Miriam!" In a fury Paul catches her in his arms and puts his mouth on her face in "a kiss of rage." This is their first real quarrel and the day ends badly because of it.

Another time Paul takes Clara to the theatre, and when she appears dressed in a low - cut gown of some clinging green stuff, he is wild with desire for her. He misses his train home because the play ends late, so Clara invites him to spend the night at her house. Of course her mother is there to chaperone, which prevents the couple from actually sleeping together, as they would like to, but before the night is out Paul steals downstairs, where he finds Clara undressing on the hearthrug. In an ecstasy of love and passion he clasps her to him. It is "a moment intense almost to agony," and she willingly lets him "adore her and tremble with joy of her," for it heals her "hurt pride." The next morning at breakfast he proposes to Clara's mother that she and Clara be his guests on a short trip to the seashore, which he will pay for with some of the proceeds of his painting - sales. To his surprise and delight, Mrs. Radford seems likely to agree to go.

Comment

So far Paul's relationship with Clara is everything that his relationship with Miriam was not, just as Clara herself is everything that Miriam was not. His comments to Miriam about the necessity for sexual passion, for "the real flame of feeling through another person," are significant in this connection, for his belief that such passion is essential to true growth is behind both his breakup with Miriam and his affair with Clara. It is important to note that Paul believes his mother to have been capable of this kind of passion (of which Miriam is capable), and indeed that he sees that it was this which "bound" her to his father. Perhaps he unconsciously recognizes, too, that it is a kind of perversion of sexual passion which has always been behind her hostility to Miriam and her possessiveness toward her sons.

It is interesting, at any rate, that Paul lapses into his father's dialect after making love to Clara. Despite the hatred between these two, the profound sexual identification of son with father, so necessary for a boy's emotional health, has taken place. The situation of the Morels is, in fact, the classic situation of the Oedipus complex as Freud described it. And as we noted earlier, Lawrence was fairly familiar -through Frieda - with many of Freud's theories at the time when he wrote *Sons and Lovers*.

CHAPTER THIRTEEN: BAXTER DAWES

Shortly after Paul's evening at the theatre with Clara he meets her husband, Baxter Dawes, in a pub one day. Evidently Dawes, or a friend of his, saw the couple leaving the theatre that night, and he begins making insulting **allusions** to Paul and Clara's relationship. Obviously he is jealous, but Paul cannot stand his needling and his insults to Clara. At last he makes a remark which causes Paul to "throw half a glass of beer in his face." But through the "chucker - out" ("bouncer") ejects him from the tavern, Dawes swears that he'll be revenged on Paul. Clara is much concerned by all this, but when she advises Paul that her husband will kill him if he doesn't carry some kind of weapon with which to protect himself, the young man simply laughs at her forebodings.

In the meantime, Dawe's hostility is becoming increasingly irksome. He takes every opportunity to annoy and threaten Paul, and since both work in the same factory, he has many such opportunities indeed. Finally Mr. Jordan, the boss, is obliged to fire him, and even (because Dawes angrily resists his attempts to order him off the premises) to bring a suit for assault against him. The suit, however, is lost when Paul testifies in court about his relationship with Clara, and both Mr. Jordan and Clara end up quite annoyed with Paul, Jordan for losing him the case, and Clara for dragging her name into the whole unsavory affair.

Lately some of Paul's ardor for Clara seems to have cooled. In a conversation with his mother he complains that "I think there must be something the matter with me, that I can't love. When she's there, as a rule, I do love her. Sometimes when I see her just as the woman, I love her, mother; but then, when she talks and criticizes, I often don't listen to her . . . why - why don't I want to marry her or anybody? I feel sometimes as if I wronged my women, mother." And of course, his trouble is - as Lawrence himself explained in his prospectus of the novel - that his intense attachment to his mother keeps him from properly loving any other woman.

Despite Paul's growing coolness, though, Clara is more passionately in love with him than ever. It maddens her when he ignores her, or is matter - of - fact with her, during the day, at work, and she lives, increasingly, for the nights, when desire still brings them together. Even then, however, Lawrence says, "Clara was not there for him, only a woman, warm, something he loved and almost worshipped, there in the dark." But in another passage of intense lyricism, in which he describes the aftermath of Paul and Clara's lovemaking, Lawrence summarizes some of his central ideas about sex: ". . . after such an evening they both were very still, having known the immensity of passion. They felt small, half afraid, childish, and wondering, like Adam and Eve when they lost their innocence and realized the magnificence of the power which drove them out of Paradise and across of great night and the great day of humanity. It was for each of them an initiation and a satisfaction. To know their own nothingness, to know the tremendous living flood which carried them always, gave them rest within themselves."

Despite this profound fulfillment, however, Clara is not perfectly satisfied with their relationship. She begins to fret that Paul does not really know or care for her, personally, and she begins, almost as Miriam did, to long for something more personal and permanent, perhaps marriage, though she insists that she wouldn't want to marry Paul even if she could. In the spring they go to the seashore together, for weekends, chaperoned by Clara's mother though they live there "as man and wife." Their nights are still happy, but during the day Paul longs to be free of Clara, and she senses his longing. "It seems," she complains, "as if you only loved me at night - as if you didn't love me in the day time." "The night is free to you," he answers. "In the daytime I want to be by myself. . . . Lovemaking stifles me in the daytime." "But it needn't be always love - making," she objects. "It always is," he replies, "when you and I are together."

Thus there is now a "battle" between them just as there had been a battle between Paul and Miriam. Clara knows she never "fully" has him. Some part, "big and vital in him," she has no hold over. And Paul knows, too, that she holds herself "still as Mrs. Dawes." She doesn't love Dawes, never has loved him, but she believes he loves her, at least depends on her. She feels "a certain surety about him that she never felt with Paul Morel." Because of this Paul and Clara gradually drift further apart. Even their lovemaking grows "more mechanical, without the marvelous glamour," and they take to a kind of wanton thrill - seeking in their sexual relationship which is far removed from the profound desire that originally brought them together.

One night, as Paul is on his way home from seeing Clara, Baxter Dawes waylays him in a lonely field and begins beating him up. At first stunned and fearful, Paul is soon aroused to defend himself, and he feels his body instinctively fighting back, his hands blindly fastened around Dawes' throat. "He was a pure instinct, without reason or feeling. His body, hard and wonderful in itself, cleaved against the struggling body of the other man; not a muscle in him relaxed. He was quite unconscious, only his body had taken upon itself to kill this other man." Suddenly he realizes what he is doing, however, and lets go of Dawes, full of "wonder and misgiving." Then Dawes turns furiously on him again, and with his fists and feet knocks the lighter, younger man unconscious. When Paul awakens he finds himself lying in the snow, in agony. He manages to drag himself home, and in the morning he tells his mother what happened. His shoulder is dislocated, and on the second day acute bronchitis sets in too. The family says publicly that he was in a bicycle accident, but his mother tells him: "now I should have done with them all," and Paul agrees. Though both Clara and Miriam come to see him, he can respond to neither of them: his thoughts and feelings have reverted to his mother once more, for she is "pale as death now, and very thin. She would sit and look at him, then away into space. There was something between them that neither dared mention." The unmentionable secret between Paul and his mother is Mrs. Morel's increasingly frightening ill health. She is "ill, distant, quiet, shadowy." Paul is "terrified of something; he dared not look at her." Her eyes seem to "grow darker, her face more waxen," though she drags about her work as usual. In the spring, Paul goes off for a four - day holiday with a friend, while his mother goes to nearby Sheffield to spend a week with her daughter Annie. But when Paul arrives in Sheffield for the last few days of the week, he finds his mother in bed, hopelessly ill. The Sheffield doctor has found that she has a tumour - probably malignant - which she had known about for months but revealed to no one. Paul is shocked, frightened, despairing. As he helps her down to tea, he thinks that "her eyes [are] so blue - such a wonderful forget-me-not blue! . . . if only they had been of a different colour he could have borne it better."

Paul arranges for a doctor to come down from Nottingham to Sheffield for a consultation. The expense is enormous - eight guineas - but he is willing to foot any such bills that may arise. The doctor concurs with the diagnosis of a tumour but declares that Mrs. Morel is too ill for an operation. The only hope is to "sweal" (melt) the growth away. But this also proves impossible, and it is soon obvious to all that Gertrude Morel is dying. She stays for two months with Annie, in Sheffield, and then, since she is fretting for her own things, her own old familiar surroundings, her agonized family brings her home to die.

Comment

The three main dramatic elements of this chapter - the disintegration of Paul's relationship with Clara, his fight with Baxter Dawes, and his mother's illness - are all of equal importance in the young man's emotional and intellectual development. Just as his relationship with Miriam had collapsed because it was all spiritual, so Paul's relationship with Clara now collapses because it has become all physical. Though his body adores Clara, Paul's mind is not very fully attuned to hers - still belongs to his mother in fact - and both are dissatisfied by their "daytime" relationship, Clara because there isn't enough of it, and Paul because there's too much of it. This being the case, the Baxter Dawes situation, which might certainly have been handled more skillfully by Paul had he so desired, (he could, for instance, have insisted on Clara getting a divorce, as Lawrence himself made Frieda get a divorce) proves to be a way out for the young man.

Dawes, a man rather like Walter Morel - uneducated, a commoner, driven by marital failure and frustration to drinking and bullying - ends up having a curiously ambiguous relationship with Paul (as we shall see in the next chapter); their relationship begins, as does Paul's and his father's, with pure hatred on both sides. In this sense it almost seems as though Paul, in his affair with Clara, a married, older woman with a Walter Morel - like husband, is acting out his unfulfillable sexual passion for his mother. Once the whole drama, including the defeat of the father - figure, is fully enacted, however, Paul no longer feels any emotional need for Clara. And when his mother, from whom this psychodrama has not succeeded in freeing him, summons him once more, through the mechanism of her illness, he returns heart and soul to her, the original heroine of his fantasies.

As for Gertrude Morel's illness, we know from Lawrence's letter to Garnett that he intended it to be partly psychosomatic in origin, a mechanism, as we have said, for maintaining control over her straying son. In holding this view Lawrence was not being entirely idiosyncratic: a number of subsequent psychoanalysts, including the break - away Freudians Groddeck and Wilhelm Reich, have thought cancer to be basically psychosomatic, a kind of disease of the soul, and it is undeniable that to the literary mind the concept of deadly, uncontrollable, malignant growth must always be an apt physical **metaphor** for mental disorder.

CHAPTER FOURTEEN: THE RELEASE

One day the Sheffield doctor mentions casually to Paul that a Nottingham man named Baxter Dawes has been brought to the local fever hospital with a bad case of typhoid. Out of curiosity Paul goes to see him, and surprisingly enough the two rivals become rather friendly. The next time Paul sees Clara he tells her what has happened - where Baxter is, how he is, etc. She is startled and her face goes pale. "Is he very bad?" she asks guiltily. "He has been," Paul replies. "He's mending now." But despite their politeness, the thought of Baxter creates a further "hostility between them." And the first chance she gets, Clara goes to Sheffield to see her husband. Though their meeting is not a success, she gets a certain pleasure out of "serving him across an insuperable distance." Proud as she is, she wants to do penance.

In the meantime, Mrs. Morel's condition gradually deteriorates. She and Paul are "afraid of each other." They both know that she is dying, but they keep up "a pretence of cheerfulness." At night he works in her room "mechanically, producing good stuff without knowing what he was doing." But "they were both afraid of the veils that were ripping between them." Other times, for long hours, it seems, Gertrude Morel lies still and silent, her mouth set in a grim, stubborn line, thinking of the past and fighting against "the great cry" that is "tearing from her." Paul can never forget "that hard, utterly lonely and stubborn clenching of her mouth which persisted for weeks." As for his mother, she thinks "of the pain, of the morphia, of the next day; hardly ever of the death. . . . Blind, with her face shut hard and blind, she was pushed towards the door."

Around this time, in November, Paul takes Clara to the sea - shore for her birthday. But it is a cold and desolate weekend they spend, talking about death on the darkened beach. "There are different ways of dying," Paul tells Clara. "My father's people are frightened, and have to be hauled out of life into death like cattle into a slaughter - house, pulled by the neck; but my mother's people are pushed from behind, inch by inch. They are stubborn people, and won't die." Clara is terrified by all this talk, and frightened, too, because Paul seems "scarcely aware of her existence." They can no longer make love at all, he is so preoccupied with his mother's sickness, and indeed for a long time their love - making has been hopelessly unsatisfactory, for Clara, in Paul's arms, feels as though she is in the embrace of death itself, so cruel and indifferent is he now.

Mrs. Morel's sufferings are terrible. Paul and Annie are almost hysterical with horror and fear; yet she seems unable to die. Day after anguished day her pitifully wasted body clings to life. Finally, one night Paul takes all the sleeping pills in the house and crushes them together in Mrs. Morel's bedtime milk. When she complains of its bitterness, he explains that it is a new sleeping draught, and she, trusting as a child, accepts his explanation. After a terrible night and day in which she falls into a coma and horrifies Paul and Annie with the loud, irregular, rasping sound of her breathing, Gertrude Morel at last dies. Later, when Paul goes up to her room, where she is laid out, to look at her, he sees that she is lying "like a girl asleep and dreaming of her love . . . her face . . . young, her brow clear and white as if life had never touched it."

Walter Morel is pathetically afraid of his wife's corpse. But he too takes his leave of her, feeling, like Paul, that she somehow looks like his young wife again. The next day, in a tremendous rainstorm, Gertrude Morel is buried. Now Paul goes from friend to friend, seeking solace and finding it nowhere. At Christmas he goes down to the seaside to stay with Baxter Dawes. When Clara comes to see him and Baxter there, they realize that all is over between them. Paul now seem singularly shallow and fickle to Clara, and Baxter, in contrast, seem solid and manly. When Paul has left, Clara stays with her husband. As they stare out the window at the sea, he asks her hoarsely "Do you want to come back to me?" And she, in an ecstasy of remorse and perhaps love, replies "Take me back! Take me back!"

Comment

Death at last accomplishes what life could not contrive to do: it frees Paul from his mother's imprisoning love. But now that he is free, as we shall see in the next chapter, the young man hardly knows what to do with himself, for the unique characteristic of his Oedipal prison was its attractiveness. And surely, in addition, the long slow horror of Gertrude Morel's death, as it is vividly related by Lawrence (a faithful description of his own mother's last sickness, incidentally) is one of the most unforgettable records of a mortal illness in literature. Lawrence also wrote a series of poems on the same subject, many of them even dealing with the same scenes (such as the one in which a strand of his mother's gray hair floats up the chimney into the blackness), many of which are equally poignant and vivid. This last crisis in his relationship with his mother forces Paul (as it forced Lawrence) to confront two major unpleasant realities: the reality of death, and the reality of his dependence on his mother. The first of these, of course, must eventually be accommodated in Paul's philosophy, as it must in all men's. The second, though, is a weakness of his own which he must conquer as part of the "growing up" that, at the age of twenty - four, he has yet to do. It is interesting to note, in connection with the problem of death, that Walter Morel is in certain respects even less able than Paul to face the reality of Gertrude Morel's death. As he was when William died, Walter Morel is overwhelmed by his wife's death, reduced to a pathetic and fearful creature. Unlike Paul, he has not even the spiritual resources to have a "soul - crisis." Having lived a life of the purest physicality, his reaction is now that of an animal - dumb, pained and uncomprehending.

The other main event of this chapter, Clara's return to her husband, is in a sense a natural consequence of Paul's mother's death, for as Lawrence explained in his letter to Garnett, Mrs.

Morel begins to die in part to divert her son from his interest in other women, and in part because she sees she cannot much longer so divert him. In any case, as we pointed out in the last comment, Paul has finished his enactment of the little Oedipal psychodrama between him, Clara and Baxter Dawes, and there is hardly any other course open to him now but to return Clara to her husband.

CHAPTER FIFTEEN: DERELICT

After the death of his mother, everything seems to have "gone smash" for Paul, including his relationship with Clara. Even his painting fails him; his last satisfactory picture was finished on the day his mother died. So he is "always in the town, at one place or another, drinking, knocking about with the men he knows. It really wearies him. . . . Everything seems so different, so unreal."

One day, as he is passing out of the Unitarian Church where he has just happened to stop by for a service, he meets Miriam. In his misery and despair, he has thought of Miriam lately, wondering if marriage to her and "the begetting of children" might help him to "live" and carry on his mother's spirit better even than painting. He had rejected the idea at once, but now, in desperation, he turns to her for comfort and invites her to supper. As usual, her consuming interest in him is flattering, yet there is the same old tension between them. Paul notices that though her curls are still "fine and free," her face is "much older, the brown throat much thinner." She seems "old to him, older than Clara. Her bloom of youth [has] quickly gone. A sort of stiffness, almost of woodenness, [has] come upon her." Finally, as he had known all along, the relationship with Miriam is hopeless. She cannot give herself to him completely, nor can she claim his body as she must, if she is to be his wife. They embrace, but neither is satisfied. For her, there is "the anguished sweetness of self - sacrifice. For him, the hate and misery of another failure."

When Paul takes Miriam home that night, they say goodbye to each other coolly. Miriam wonders where Paul will go now, and what he will do. She thinks that he has "no religion," and cares only for "the moment's attraction," yet she is still certain that when he has "had enough" he will "give in and come to her."

As for Paul, as he walks back to town in the dark he feels himself surrounded by "the vastness and terror of the immense night which is roused and stirred for a brief while by the day, but which returns, and will remain at last eternal, holding everything in its silence and its living gloom. . . . Who could say," he thinks, "that his mother had lived and did not live? She had been in one place, and was in another; that was all. And his soul could not leave her, wherever she was. Now she was gone abroad into the night, and he was with her still. They were together. But yet there was his body, his chest, that leaned against the stile, his hands on the wooden bar. They seemed something. Where was he? - one tiny upright speck of flesh, less than an ear of wheat lost in the field. He could not bear it. On every side the immense dark silence seemed pressing him, so tiny a spark, into extinction, and yet, almost nothing, he could not be extinct. . . . 'Mother!' he whimpered, 'mother!' . . ." And yet he will not give in to utter despair. "Turning sharply, he walked towards the city's gold phosphorescence. His fists were shut, his mouth set fast. He would not take that direction, to the darkness, to follow her. He walked towards the faintly humming, glowing town, quickly."

Comment

In this magnificent, and famous, last passage of *Sons and Lovers*, Lawrence describes Paul's re-awakening to life from the blank and total despair of his grief for his mother. The **imagery** is obvious and simple - a man is a minuscule living thing, "less than an ear of wheat," amid the lifeless darkness of the universe. He is "a tiny spark," and the sun and moon are "a few bright grains," they and he alone alive, organic, in the blackness. Yet though there is "at the core a nothingness," man and moon and sun are "not nothing." As he does throughout *Sons and Lovers* - and his other works too - Lawrence, at the end, even amid the bleakness of death and desolation, must affirm the higher, greater reality of life, the life into which what Wordsworth called "a universe of death" is mysteriously urged. At last everything must fall before this final, triumphant reality of life. He who would deny the life in himself - as Miriam, for instance, does, in denying her own natural sexuality - becomes prematurely aged and "wooden," deathlike, as Miriam has. Even art, always, Paul's greatest delight and consolation, is less important. "Painting is not living," he says to himself, and as between carrying on his mother's "effort" of life through painting or through begetting children, the latter is preferable. It is closer to the basic, affirmative reality of the flesh -the process of begetting, birth, and growth which living things can oppose to death. Art, painting, has its own kind of immortality too, of course, an immortality which Lawrence, as an artist, would have been the last to deny. But basically Lawrence was, as we have already seen, a romantic, for whom the flux, the striving, the tumultuous life - urge, the "quick" of the universe, was the final reality, the ultimate good. Thus *Sons and Lovers* concludes with Paul walking "quickly" - a significant pun - towards the town before him, the town which is "faintly humming" and "glowing" with its own mysterious and various life. He is mature at last; he has passed through the final crisis in his growth. He has faced death and separation from his mother and having overcome these he is ready at last to try his single strength against the world.

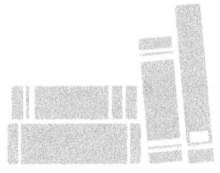

SONS AND LOVERS

CHARACTER ANALYSES

PAUL MOREL

The central character of *Sons and Lovers* is a good portrait of the young D.H. Lawrence himself. Paul is a light, quick, slender boy, tall, with a shock of reddish, light - brown hair and, later on, a mustache like the young Lawrence's. His "keen, aloof young body" - as it seems to Miriam - is wiry and expressive. His hands are mobile and display the same sensitivity and alertness as his mobile face. His features are good but "rough," like those of Lawrence himself, because - like Lawrence - he is "a man of the people, a common man."

From childhood on Paul is especially sensitive, artistic and imaginative, and he becomes extraordinarily dependent on his mother, a highly intelligent woman with an unusually strong and vivid personality. Thus, when he gets older and begins to have important relationships with girls, his attachment to her prevents him from loving them as fully as he feels he should. Lawrence, in his letter to Garnett (cf. the Introduction) thoroughly analyzed this central difficulty of Paul's, a difficulty which is the mainspring of the novel, its focal conflict. His description of Paul's problem and of his intense, distorted relationship with his mother sounds like a straightforward description of the classic Freudian Oedipus complex. As we know, Lawrence - through Frieda - was roughly acquainted with Freud's theories so it is not surprising that his characterization of Paul, in *Sons and Lovers*, should have been one of the first Freudian "case studies" - if not the first - to appear in an English novel.

But besides being a son, and a lover, Paul is also and very importantly an artist, and Lawrence's story of his boyhood and youth is, as we have seen, a brilliant bildungsroman in which the development of a sensitive talented child into a mature artist of potential genius is carefully and deliberately traced. Thus we see Paul being stimulated and encouraged both by his mother and Miriam. His mother "urges" him toward success for her sake - so that she can live through him - while Miriam eagerly, flatteringly, encourages his talent for his own sake because she is self - sacrificingly in love with his genius and quickness. Yet whatever the respective motivations of the two women, it is clear from Paul's character and from his relationships with them that without their help he might not achieve the artistic success that we feel he is destined to achieve, just as D. H. Lawrence himself might not have achieved his artistic success either so early or so fully without the help and encouragement of his mother, Jessie Chambers and, later, his wife Frieda.

A final point about Paul's personality: Paul is a volatile, gregarious, likeable young man with, indeed, much of Lawrence's own charm and mercurial "gift for life." He is adored by the girls at Jordan's, loved by all the Leiverses, and generally a social success with most young people his own age. The two girls with whom he has important relationships in the book, Miriam and Clara, fall desperately in love with him, and in the end it is he who rejects them, not they who reject him. This is a departure from the pattern of most bildungsroman where the hero (cf. Mann's Tonio Kroeger) often fruitlessly spends his love and his genius in the pursuit of a rather worthless girl who couldn't care less about him. Interestingly, the one person who actively dislikes Paul in *Sons and Lovers* is Baxter Dawes, who is not only roused to sexual jealousy by Paul's success with his estranged wife Clara, but who has, long before the Paul - Clara affair, been enraged by the way in which Paul's "impersonal gaze of an artist" seems to penetrate and evaluate him.

GERTRUDE MOREL

Just as Paul Morel was an accurate and detailed portrait of the young Lawrence, Gertrude Morel is an excellent portrait of Lydia Lawrence, the author's mother. A strong - willed, refined, puritanical, middle - class girl who has been shocked and disappointed by her marriage to a miner, a man of a class lower than hers, Gertrude Morel is a fascinating compound of faults and virtues. Her virtues are, perhaps, more obviously stressed in the book. Hard - working, thrifty, uncomplaining, and, most important, possessing exceptional intelligence and strength of will, Gertrude Morel makes the most of the difficult situation in which she finds herself. Her household is "coolly and competently run." Her children, like the Lawrence children, are always proud of their home, despite its shabbiness and the family's lack of money for expensive improvements. Most of all, Gertrude Morel devotes herself passionately to her children, especially her sons, seeing to it that they have every advantage she can give them, making the most of every talent with which they are endowed, relentlessly driving them onward and upward, out of the mire in which they find themselves, into a higher class, a better life.

But if this "urging" of her sons toward success is, in a sense, Gertrude Morel's greatest virtue, it also involves her greatest fault, for in the course of her intense and passionate devotion to them she arouses in her sons, as we have seen, a reciprocal attachment which is essentially unhealthy. Thus, although she succeeds in making her boys succeed, she fails to establish them, as a mother should, as self-sufficient and independent individuals capable of living their own lives and loving their own loves without constant reference to her judgments and feelings. In this sense we might say that Gertrude Morel suffers as severely from a kind of "Jocasta complex" as Paul and William suffer from Oedipus complexes. It is Gertrude, after all, who seductively tells Paul that "I never really had a husband," and Gertrude who has been driven, by her disappointment in her real, lawful husband, to make her sons into miniature husband-figures from their earliest childhood.

Thus, although we warm to her intelligence, her wit, and her brave struggle against poverty, we often feel that there is something sinister about Paul's mother. Even when she seems to be most loving, as in the scene with Paul on the stairs (on the Friday night when the bread burns), we sense that she is somehow corrupting him with her love. Even when her actions seem most justified, as when she is shocked by Walter Morel's irresponsible drunkenness and thriftlessness, we feel that there is something hard, unyielding, and unsympathetic in her, a righteousness and puritanism which is at least in part responsible for the very drunkenness and brutishness to which it is opposed. Gertrude Morel was an intense young woman, capable, as Paul recognizes, of true sexual passion, of "the real, real flame of feeling through another person." But when her relationship with her husband - for whatever reasons - failed to ripen into a permanent bond of love, her passionate nature shifted focus and fixed on her sons as objects of a most intense passion. In this rather morbid fixation, Gertrude Morel partially created yet partially destroyed their talents and their hopes.

WALTER MOREL

Lawrence's attitude toward Walter Morel is strikingly ambivalent throughout *Sons and Lovers*, just as his attitude toward his own father was essentially ambivalent. The Lawrence children "hated" their father during their growing - up years. In contrast to Lydia Lawrence, Arthur Lawrence, like Walter Morel, was coarse, "brutish," unrefined, and uneducated. Thus Walter Morel is generally shown as drunken, brutal, thriftless and often irresponsible toward his family. His intemperateness and commonness, in fact, are the cause of the rift with his wife, the rift which turns her passion so irrevocably toward her sons. On the other hand, however, Lawrence recognized the good sides of his father, and he included them in his portrait of Walter Morel. The black - bearded miner is a handy man around the house, a strong and skillful workman with a jolly temper and a habit of singing cheerfully when he is doing little jobs of carving or repairing. When Gertrude Morel first meets him, furthermore, he is handsome and vital looking, gregarious and well - mannered. In his later novels, Lawrence gradually emphasized these aspects of his father more than he had in *Sons and Lovers*, but even in this early work they are undeniably present and should not be overlooked by readers.

Another aspect of Walter Morel that should not be overlooked is his increasing pathos toward the end of the book. As he ages and is "cast off" by his wife, Morel, for all his hard drinking and his braggadocio, becomes little more than a "husk" of a man. He ages badly, becoming alternately "mean" and "scared" in response to new developments in the family. Yet though Lawrence often describes these new characteristics of Morel's rather scornfully, if we "trust the tale" and "not the teller" (as Lawrence himself admonished critics to do) we invariably sympathize with the miner. We have already felt the subtle ways in which Mrs. Morel is sinister toward her sons. Now we feel, too, the ways in which she has a sinister effect on her husband: her independence, her pride, her indifference, more than anything else, finally deprive him of his strength and his manhood, at least as much as his own animalism and lack of self - awareness have deprived him of his family's love.

MIRIAM LEIVERS

One of the most interesting characters in the book is undoubtedly Miriam Leivers, Lawrence's fictionalized portrait of his first love, Jessie Chambers. Jessie herself, as we have noted, was quite resentful of the picture Lawrence drew of her here: she felt it was thoroughly unfair and inaccurate, and years later she even wrote her own book of reminiscences to correct the false impressions she thought the young Lawrence gave of her. Certainly there is no denying that Jessie Chambers, like Miriam in the novel, was Gertrude Morel - Lydia Lawrence's most pathetic victim, for without gaining any of the strength that William and Paul undoubtedly got from their mother's love, Miriam - Jessie was the object of its most destructive power. According to Jessie, even after Mrs. Lawrence's death the author, still under her spell, portrayed Miriam insultingly and unrealistically so as to make his mother seem superior.

Actually, Lawrence's portrait of Miriam is not so negative as Jessie Chambers thought. Moreover, however inaccurate the characterization may have been in relation to its original, Jessie forgot, or failed to consider, that Lawrence was writing not history, but fiction. As a purely fictional characterization, then, his Miriam is fascinating and unforgettable. Intense, mystical, religiously inclined from early childhood, the Miriam Leivers of *Sons and Lovers* is a beautiful girl with black curls "fine and free" and the attraction of "a shy, wild, quiveringly sensitive thing." Paul is flattered and fascinated by her mind, and by her interest in his mind, for as Mrs. Morel observes, Miriam seems to want to "absorb" all of him in her almost fanatic enthusiasm for his genius. Her intensity reveals itself not only in this, however, but also in her physical fear and awkwardness, a sense of strain and stiffness in the way she stands and walks. Later, when she and Paul grow up more and are confronted with the issue of sex, Miriam's religious and "spiritual" proclivities prevent her from being able to relax sexually, from being able to yield herself to the body's "impersonal swoon" of desire. She is always frigid, "clenched" rigidly against Paul, as she had been stiff with strain and foreboding before the physical world - the simple world of games and swings - when she was still a child. It is finally this stiffness, this "woodenness," this inability to relax and give herself to ordinary life, physical and social, that turns Paul against Miriam, for though he is plainly under his mother's influence in breaking off the relationship, it is rather clear, too, that Paul, with his gift for the "real real flame" of physical as well as mental life, could never find any kind of ultimate happiness in a marriage to someone as purely spiritual as Miriam.

CLARA DAWES

The sensual, slightly older woman with whom Paul finally discovers the joys of "passion" was probably modeled on several different women in Lawrence's own life. One was Louie Burrows, a student-teacher to whom the young writer was engaged for a time. Another was an older married woman (unidentified, except speculatively, by biographers) with whom he is supposed to have had an intense affair at one point. And a third is Frieda Weekley, the slightly older German woman whom he finally married in 1914, after living two years with her on the continent and in England. There is no doubt, certainly, that Clara took her physical characteristics from Frieda, who was large, blonde, sensual and "splendid." But beside being physically "superb," Clara is a suffragette, an advocate of women's rights, a type of whom Lawrence became increasingly disapproving as the years went by. In the novel, however, the young author does not give too much attention to this interest of Clara's. She is seen more usually as (a) a victim of industrialism, a magnificent animal whose magnificence and pride have been partially "bent" and broken by the machines society forces her to tend; and (b) a sensual creature, a ripely responsive woman, with whom Paul first becomes aware of the mysterious generative power of the universe as it is embodied in sex.

WILLIAM MOREL

Paul's older brother, a handsome and intelligent young man who combines his father's gregariousness and physical magnetism with his mother's intelligence and will power. As Lawrence noted in his letter to Garnett, William "gives his sex to a fribble," and in thus "going for passion" suffers a split between his urgent, young, masculine desires and the high spiritual standards his mother has instilled in him, a "split" that ultimately kills him.

LOUISA LILY DENYS WESTERN

("Gypsy"): William's fiancee, the shallow, superficial, beautiful "fribble" to whom he gives his first, intense sexual passion.

Within three months after his death, as William had predicted, she is enjoying herself at dances and parties as if he had never existed.

ARTHUR AND ANNIE MOREL

Paul's other brother and his only sister in the book. Arthur, younger than Paul, is spoiled, handsome, restless and rather irresponsible. Eventually he gets his girlfriend pregnant and is forced to settle down. Though he does this against his will, he ends up making a reasonably "good job" of it. Annie, Paul's slightly older sister, is rather a neutral character, with few traits beyond general intelligence and sympathy with Paul being ascribed to her.

BAXTER DAWES

A fascinating, Walter Morel - like character, Clara Dawes' husband. Thirty - nine years old and a failure at the Jordan factory, Dawes, like Morel, drinks heavily and bullies his wife. After an early relationship of "pure hate," he and Paul, strangely, become friends, and, rather unbelievably, they more or less settle the ultimate fate of Clara between them.

MR. JORDAN AND FANNIE

Paul's associates on his job. Mr. Jordan, his boss, is a white - mustached, red - faced little man who actually treats the young man quite decently after a rather inauspicious beginning. Fannie, the hunchback, is one of Paul's special friends among the factory girls.

THE LEIVERSES

Miriam's parents, brothers and sister. Her mother, Mrs. Leivers, a religious, delicate, spiritual woman - much like her daughter - is one of Paul's particular favorites at Willey Farm. Edgar, the oldest son, is a strong, sensible young man who becomes one of his closest men - friends, and to whom he turns for friendship at a time when his relationship with Miriam is going sour.

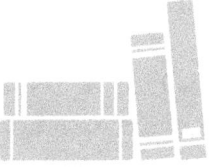

SONS AND LOVERS

CRITICAL COMMENTARY

EARLY REACTIONS TO LAWRENCE

Quite early in his career - indeed, almost from the day when Ford Madox Ford published his first poems in a place of honor in *The English Review* - D. H. Lawrence was considered a genius by various influential members of the literary establishment. Ford thought his first novel, *The White Peacock*, a work of genius, but he also thought it had "every fault that the English novel can have," for the young writer was as yet undisciplined and unformed. *The Trespasser*, too, was given this kind of ambiguous critical reception. But *Sons and Lovers* was a rather different case, for this autobiographical, Freudian story of a working-class boy's growth to maturity in the English Midlands was quickly recognized as an extraordinary effort, a major novel in its own right, and the first mature achievement of its twenty - six - year - old author. Even Henry James, a perceptive critic but one in whom we would hardly expect to find an early and enthusiastic Lawrentian, ranked Lawrence, on the basis of this book, as one of the most promising novelists of the younger generation, although in comparison to writers like Gilbert Cannan, Hugh Walpole and Compton Mackenzie (now all virtually unknown),

James found the young author of *Sons and Lovers* hanging "in the dusty rear." Still the general reaction of most reviewers was summarized by John Macy, a contemporary critic, who wrote in the introduction to the *Boni and Liveright* edition of 1922 that "here is . . . a masterpiece in which every sentence counts, a book crammed with significant thought and beautiful, arresting phrases, the work of a singular genius whose gifts are more richly various than those of any other young English novelist."

THE SWING OF THE PENDULUM

Within Lawrence's lifetime, however, some critics - especially Lawrence's friends and partisans -began to think more highly of his other books, *The Rainbow, Women in Love, The Plumed Serpent* and *Lady Chatterley*, each of which had its special enthusiasts. This tendency continued - and has continued among influential Lawrentians like F. R. Leavis and Harry T. Moore - even up to the present day. At the same time there was also beginning to develop a reaction against all of Lawrence's work, a reaction which was in full swing at the time of his death and in the two decades immediately following. A Lawrence admirer like Horace Gregory could remark, then, in the course of one of the first positive critical studies of the author, that Lawrence's novels have "dated" considerably in the years since they were first written. And even F. R. Leavis, later to become England's leading Lawrentian, could comment, in 1930, that "Everyone I have discussed it with agrees with me in finding [*Sons and Lovers*] difficult to get through."

TWENTY YEARS LATER

By 1950, twenty years after the author's death, the trend had started to reverse itself, and Lawrence once more began to receive the critical appreciation that was his due. Two writers who led the new movement were F. R. Leavis - whose *D. H. Lawrence, Novelist* has probably been more influential than any other single study of the author's work - and Harry T. Moore, Lawrence's most thorough and scholarly biographer, whose *The Life and Works of D. H. Lawrence* was the first comprehensive critical biography to be written about the author. Both these men, but especially Leavis, tended to rate *Sons and Lovers* less highly than the general public does. Leavis, in particular, asserted unequivocally that *The Rainbow* and *Women in Love* were Lawrence's masterpieces, works of profound social and moral analysis which placed their author directly in "the great tradition" of the English novel. Most subsequent critics of Lawrence have followed in Dr. Leavis' footsteps, granting the greatness of much of Lawrence's other work but always insisting on the ultimate superiority of *The Rainbow* and *Women in Love* (with the notable exception of W. Y. Tindall, who finds *The Plumed Serpent* and *Sons and Lovers* the author's finest achievements).

RECENT ANALYSES OF SONS AND LOVERS

Despite this general critical accord which has been reached, a number of commentators have undertaken to analyze and evaluate *Sons and Lovers*, especially in the last decade, when so much Lawrence criticism has been written. These writers include Seymour Betsky, Graham Hough, Anthony Beal and Ronald Draper. Betsky, in an essay written in 1953 for *The Achievement of D. H. Lawrence*, a collection of essays about the author edited by Harry T. Moore and Frederick J. Hoffman, discussed the uniquely Lawrentian "rhythm" of the book, a rhythm of tension and relaxation in the central relationships which, Betsky points out, was to become the author's typical substitute for conventional plot development. Following Leavis, however, Betsky feels that, brilliant though *Sons and Lovers* is, it does not explore the social condition of contemporary England in enough depth to rival the achievement of the later *Women in Love*. "Had Lawrence developed the subordinate **theme** of *Sons and Lovers*, as he does in his later work, that novel might have explored the plight of his English civilization," he writes. "[It] might then have been a novel of major proportions. . . . In *Sons and Lovers* Paul is the artist who earns his self - identity by defining himself against his complex society: home, the mining community, industrial England, religious belief and action, the educational system, the "natural world" and the farming community. [But] that **theme** is kept rigorously subordinate to the Freudian." He concludes, finally, that *Sons and Lovers*, with its heavy dependence on autobiographical material and its introspective rather than social emphasis, "is a purgation become the successful work of art. The best of Lawrence's later works are, in similar fashion, acts of purgation. But this time 'the sickness of a whole civilization' is the true theme."

THE VIEW OF HOUGH

Graham Hough, in his thorough 1956 study of Lawrence, *The Dark Sun*, agreed that *Sons and Lovers* "is a catharsis, achieved by re - living an actual experience - re - living it over and over again"; and, he added, "the achievement is a necessary preliminary to all the later work." Unlike Betsky, however, who had thought the sections dealing with Mrs. Morel were the "sharpest" parts of the novel, Hough thinks "the Paul and Miriam chapters are the essential core of *Sons and Lovers*. Adolescent love has been treated in fiction both before and since, tenderly or ironically; but never with such penetration, so little sentimentality or such honest determination to show its nature and the corruptions to which it is subject. Lawrence takes it seriously, and this is rarely done; and he treats it, under the pressure of an urgent personal necessity, from the inside." On the other hand, "the part of the book which is most contrived," he adds, "is the love affair with Clara Dawes." Nevertheless he notes that *Sons and Lovers* will remain Lawrence's "masterpiece for those who abide by the central tradition of the novel. He himself, however, tends to agree with the Leavis - Betsky critical accord that the book was only a starting point for Lawrence, a psychological experience which liberated the young author's powers for his later and greater work.

THE VIEWS OF BEAL

Anthony Beal, though like most critics he agrees with this judgment, feels, unlike Hough, that the Miriam section is the most strained part of *Sons and Lovers*. In his 1961 *Evergreen Pilot Series* study of Lawrence, he echoes Betsky's view that the depiction of the Morel family is the most dazzling achievement in the book - but he does agree with Hough on the weakness of the Clara section. "*Sons and Lovers* has been, and is likely to remain, Lawrence's most popular book," Beal notes, "and it is at its best when it is nearest the truth - in the brilliant early pages on the Morel's family life. In the second part of the book, dominated by the Miriam - Paul relationship, there is more of a sense of strain, because Lawrence is obviously still puzzling out exactly what had gone wrong between them - but the adolescent world is wonderfully evoked. The final Clara **episode** is the yeast satisfactory, but the end of the novel is redeemed by the moving account of Mrs. Morel's death."

THE VIEWS OF DRAPER

Ronald Draper, the most recent surveyor of the Lawrence canon, made in 1964, in the *Twayne English Authors Series*, a rather different judgment. "To be quite blunt about it," he writes - in contradiction to the earlier critic Betsky, who admired the portrait of Mrs. Morel - "Mrs. Morel is given over - sympathetic treatment. Te intense love that Lawrence felt for his own mother is probably responsible for a disequilibrium in a presentation of Paul's mother and father which is harmful to the main **theme** . . . too often the reader is invited to share in the conspiracy of mother and children against the husband." Like Betsky and Hough, however, Draper concludes that "the finest achievement of *Sons and Lovers* is [its] quickening truthfulness to actual life - 'the shimmering protoplasm' which Paul tries to capture in his paintings, and which is 'the real living.'" And surely there is no denying, however highly one may rate Lawrence's later novels, that few works of art 'exist' for readers as thoroughly and vividly as *Sons and Lovers* does. Here, after a series of early experiments with both prose and poetry, the young writer - still only twenty - six - years old - emerged from his apprenticeship, and the hand of the master was seen.

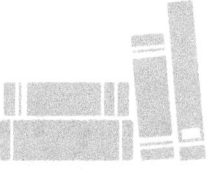

THE RAINBOW

The Rainbow is the story of three generations of the Brangwen family, a family of farmers which has held the Marsh Farm, on the Derbyshire - Nottinghamshire borders, from - it seems - time immemorial. The first Brangwen Lawrence deals with is Tom Brangwen, whom we meet when he is still in his twenties. At the beginning of the novel, he is lonely, sexually frustrated and unfulfilled. Then one day he passes a strange woman on the road and "That's her," he says involuntarily to himself; like many of Lawrence's characters, he has fallen in love or, more precisely, "recognized" the mystical "other" to whom he must be joined, at first sight. The woman is Lydia Lensky, a Polish widow who has come to this rural Midland neighborhood with her small daughter to work as a housekeeper for the local vicar. Eventually she and Tom are formally introduced; very soon he proposes to her, and they get married, though, as Anthony Beal points out, "in every way the utter foreignness between them is emphasized. It is not just that their backgrounds are so alien: they have little to talk about, and do not even take very much conscious notice of one another." Yet, after their marriage, "the hours of remoteness alternate with moments of intense consummation: 'He knew her essence . . . And he seemed to live thus in contact with her, in contact with the unknown, the unaccountable and incalculable.'"

This mysterious relationship, the first to be described in *The Rainbow* and probably the strangest in the book, is nevertheless of vital importance to the **theme** and structure of the work; it is, as it were, the model relationship of the novel, in some ways Lawrence's picture of what he considered an ideal sexual relationship - profoundly significant yet, because of the alienness of the partners, strangely impersonal and almost religious in its intensity. Because it is based on a kind of mystical magnetism of "the blood" rather than on any kind of superficial intellectual attraction, it brings Tom and Lydia into a communion with the mysterious generative forces of the universe - "the unknown, the unaccountable and the incalculable" -rather than simply into a single finite relationship with another human being.

After a while Tom and Lydia have a number of children. Yet it is not the children of their marriage on whom Lawrence focuses next, but Anna Lensky, Lydia's daughter by her first husband, who has been more or less adopted by Brangwen, and who, after various childhood and adolescent experiences, marries Will Brangwen, her step - cousin through Tom. In contrast to the mystical marriage of Tom and Lydia, the relationship of Will and Anna is perfectly ordinary - in fact, as Beal points out, theirs "stands as a picture of absolutely normal marriage against the strange, but deeper relationship between Tom and Lydia." As in all of Lawrence's male - female relationships, however, this one between Will And Anna, like that of Tom and Lydia earlier, is fraught with conflicts, a profound subterranean battle between the man and woman for ascendancy as well as the little daily battles - the disagreements and irritations which mar the surface of any marriage. In the case of Will and Anna the major struggle, which occurs quite soon after they are married, is over religion, for Will tends to be religiously inclined while Anna feels confined by the dark and limited space of the Cathedral which he loves. Later Will more or less abandons his earlier religious "ecstasies" and finds a kind of fulfillment in his craft as a carver, while Anna finds hers in bringing up her nine children. Yet both remain essentially "uncreated," for they have failed to fulfill their real potential as human beings, failed even in comparison to Tom and Lydia, who have at least attained a profoundly satisfying relationship with each other.

The last section of the novel deals with the childhood and youth of Ursula Brangwen, Will's and Anna's oldest daughter, and it is almost a kind of separate bildungsroman, a kind of female version of *Sons and Lovers*. Indeed, though Ursula is brought up in a more rural atmosphere than Lawrence and Paul More, when she is in her teens she becomes, like Lawrence himself, though not Paul, a student - teacher, then eventually a regular teacher. As a young girl she is ecstatically religious, like her father, but when she is older her intense emotions are channeled into a love affair with a young British subaltern of Polish descent, Anton Skrebensky. This affair is a rapturous idyll at first, but eventually it begins to collapse, when Ursula realizes how superficial her lover really is. When Anton goes off to war, Ursula engages in a lesbian relationship with one of her schoolmistresses, a relationship which represents, in the person of Winifred Inger who corrupts Ursula, the unnaturalness of the "modern independent young woman." Eventually Ursula is repelled by this unnaturalness, and she introduces Winifred to an uncle of hers, who manages a colliery. When he and Winifred duly marry, their union stands for all that is mechanistic and life - destroying in modern industrial society. "His real mistress [is] the machine, and the real mistress of Winfred [is] the machine," so their marriage is inevitable - and inevitably hateful to Ursula, who "once had loved them both."

After this trauma, Ursula, at loose ends, turns seriously to her teaching, which is itself another soul - destroying modern experience, in Lawrence's view. His portrayal of the huge classes of fifty or sixty children learning mechanically and through brutal discipline is frightening and unforgettable. Then, exhausted from her two years of "teaching," Ursula goes to the University of Nottingham (Lawrence's alma mater) which she finds a "warehouse of dead unreality." As Beal notes, "her young life is a pilgrim's progress of disillusionment." Finally, when Skrebensky returns to England she realizes, after briefly resuming their affair, that her relationship with him is also hopeless. Though she is pregnant she breaks off with him, and has first a miscarriage, then a nervous breakdown. Nevertheless, the book ends on a note of almost mystical hope and joy, with Ursula's vision of the rainbow that bridges heaven and earth, "symbolizing the earth's new architecture, a change of heart."

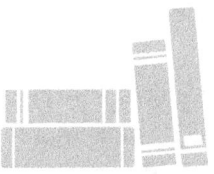

WOMEN IN LOVE

Women in Love is widely considered Lawrence's greatest novel. F.R. Leavis, for the last twenty - five years one England's foremost Lawrentians, is perhaps its most passionate advocate. He considers it Lawrence's supreme achievement and most other Lawrence critics, men like Harry Moore, Eliseo Vivas, Anthony Beal and Mark Schorer also hold this view. Though *Women in Love* was originally conceived as a sequel to *The Rainbow*, in its final form it bore little or no relationship to the preceding book, though Lawrence had actually planned a trilogy - *The Rainbow*, *Women in Love*, and *Aaron's Rod* - in the grand manner. Unlike *The Rainbow*, which was a family - chronicle type of novel *Women in Love* turned out to be a sophisticated and penetrating vision of contemporary society and, as so many critics put it, an "architectonic" masterpiece, a brilliant job of structuring and interrelating events and personalities -certainly Lawrence's greatest such job.

As its title implies, *Women In Love* is a novel about two love affairs, and, as the title also suggests, these affairs are presented rather (though only slightly) more from the female than the male point of view. The two heroines are Ursula Brangwen, the Ursula of *The Rainbow* but now entirely grown up, and her younger sister Gudrun, a brilliant, beautiful, artistic girl who appeared only briefly in the earlier novel. Except for the continuity of these characters there is little other connection between the two novels. Ursula, incidentally, with her down - to - earth common sense and wry wit, is supposed to have been modeled on the equally down - to - earth Frieda Lawrence, while the mercurial, talented Gudrun is considered a vivid portrait of the brilliant and dashing Katherine Mansfield.

The two chief male characters - Gerald Crich, a handsome, blond industrialist, a bold and inventive "captain of industry" whose soul has been subtly corrupted by the machines around which he has built his life, and Rupert Birkin, Crich's best friend, an intellectual school inspector - are supposed to have been patterned respectively (at least in part) on Katherine Mansfield's husband, J. Middleton Murry, and D. H. Lawrence himself. Certainly Birkin, with "his wonderful, desirable life - rapidity, the rare quality of an utterly desirable man; and . . . at the same time [his] ridiculous, mean effacement into a Salvator Mundi and a Sunday-school teacher, a prig of the stiffest type," has many of Lawrence's best and worst qualities, while Crich, too, does reflect some of the author's attitudes toward Murry. The physical description of Crich, however, as well as many of the external features of his life, were based on those of a Major T. P. Barber, a local Nottinghamshire gentleman and mine - owner who never condescended either to read the book or make the acquaintance of the great writer who so vividly immortalized these aspects of him.

As the book opens, Ursula and Gudrun, who have just resolved that marriage is "intolerable," attend the wedding of Gerald Crich's sister, where they meet Gerald, Rupert and Rupert's mistress, Hermione - an intellectual aristocrat based on Lady Ottoline Morrell, one of Lawrence's earliest patronesses - among other guests, and as Anthony Beal has pointed out "the rest of the novel is a working out of their relationships."

Ursula and Rupert Birkin feel an immediate kinship, but since Birkin is still involved with Hermione, nothing develops for a while. Gerald Crich and Rupert are also too immersed in London's bohemian life to see very much of the slightly provincial Brangwen girls as yet. Gradually, however, the two couples are brought together, throughout a whole vivid series of scenes, including a memorable one at Hermione's country house, where all four spend a weekend together with Hermione's brother, the bachelor M.P. "striding romantically like a Meredith hero who remembers Disraeli" and Sir Joshua, "a learned, dry Baronet of fifty, who was always making witticisms and laughing at them heartily in a harsh horse -laugh," who is like "a flat bottle, containing tabloids of compressed liberty."

Interspersed with these dazzling London and exurban scenes of intellectual and/or upper - class social life are a number of chapters dealing with the Midland mines owned by Gerald Crich's father, and the new, "modern," efficient system of production Gerald has brought to them. We see that Gerald, the powerful public man, represents "the great mechanical purpose" of the new industrial world, as opposed to the more reflective Birkin, a wholly private man, whose inclination is, like Lawrence's own, toward a religious reverence for the "organic," the precious life - principle which animates the universe. When Gerald's father dies, Gerald, who has no inner resources with which to fight off despair, turns to Gudrun for consolation, and they plunge into a passionate, though essentially barren, love affair. In the meantime, Birkin and Ursula, after a series of sometimes rather theoretical ups and downs ("'What I want is a strange conjunction with you,'" he said quietly . . . 'an equilibrium, a pure balance of two single beings: as the stars balance each other.' She looked at him. He was very earnest. . . . Yet she liked him so much. But why drag in the stars?") finally decide to get married. Theirs, unlike Gerald and Gudrun's, is to be a permanent and fruitful relationship, while Gudrun is "a born mistress" and Gerald is "a born lover."

At last the two couples decide to go together for a vacation to the Austrian Alps. When they are there, Gudrun and Gerald's relationship begins to disintegrate, as it was inevitably doomed to by its very nature. Gudrun meets Loerke, a grotesque little man, a German sculptor, who represents the classless man, the clear-sighted, sardonic artist who sees society without illusions. With him she finds the "impersonal" relationship which Birkin (and Lawrence) believes to be so important. If she cannot transcend her own "little ego" through love, in other words, as Ursula and Rupert presumably have, she can do it through art. "I and my art, they have nothing to do with each other. My art stands in another world, I am in this world," she declares.

By now Ursula and Birkin have decided to go south, to Italy. Permanently fixed in each other's orbits, they at last feel the freedom to wander where they will in search of the good life, much as Lawrence and Frieda themselves did. Left behind, Gerald and Gudrun drift hopelessly apart. One day, in a passion of jealousy, Gerald tries to kill Gudrun when he finds her walking in the snow with Loerke. When he fails, he is still "consumed by the death wish," as Anthony Beal puts it, and wandering through the icy, snow-mantled mountains - a perfect symbol of his own deathly barrenness of soul - he falls and is killed by the cold, by his own as much as nature's coldness. Lawrence, a world-traveler himself, always used geography brilliantly, and nowhere more so than here, where a sterile relationship, Gerald and Gudrun's, ends amid icy sterility, while a fertile one, Ursula and Birkin's, is transported, symbolically as well as actually, to the ripe Italian valleys of the south.

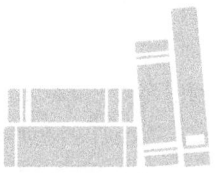

THE PLUMED SERPENT

Though many critics - especially those of the Leavis school - have a very low regard for this novel, (Leavis termed it "the least complex" and the most "difficult to get through" of all Lawrence's novels) Lawrence himself called the book, which was his last except for *Lady Chatterley*, "my most important novel, so far." It has recently come in for a good deal more interest and attention than it used to receive. W. Y. Tindall, for instance, who wrote an excellent introduction to the *Knopf* (American) edition of 1951, calls it a "splendid barbaric novel" and ranks it with *Sons and Lovers* as the author's greatest work. And indeed, despite its longueurs, the increasing tedium of its repetitive, incantatory rituals, and the occasionally fascistic sound of some of the theories it seems to propose, it has a special fascination of its own, the fascination of Lawrence the myth - maker, Lawrence the teller of tales, perhaps the most hypnotic storyteller of our time.

This is an aspect of Lawrence which was not very much in evidence throughout *Sons and Lovers* or *The Rainbow* and *Women in Love*, in which the author functioned rather more conventionally within the traditional structure of the novel, the structure of social observation and criticism that has come down to us from the eighteenth and especially the nineteenth century. But Lawrence, as he grew older, began to grow increasingly restless within the confines of this kind of nineteenth-century social **realism**. He wanted to penetrate deeper into human motives and human destinies than such a limited tracing of social patterns would allow him to go. The poetic symbolism of *The Rainbow* and *Women in Love* had been a step in the right direction. But now he began to write vividly imagined stories which might almost, for want of a better phrase, be called realistic fairy tales. Indeed, it was the very **realism** of these fairy tales which made them great, for where most fairy tales tend to be remote and dreamlike in style, the peculiarly concrete, detailed quality of Lawrence's imagination, his talent for reproducing the exact weight and sense of physical life, gave these stories the same brilliant presence of his earlier, more conventional works. "The Man Who Loved Islands," "Sun," "The Woman Who Rode Away," "The Princess," "*St. Mawr*," "The Man Who Died," and, in some respects, *Lady Chatterley's Lover*, are all examples of this paradoxically realistic vein of fantasy that Lawrence increasingly used in his later years. And certainly *The Plumed Serpent* is the most ambitious example of all.

The story of *The Plumed Serpent* is simple but boldly - perhaps too boldly - conceived. Kate Leslie, a forty-year-old Irish widow, travels to Mexico, in search of she knows not what spiritual fulfillment. Like many of Lawrence's heroines in these stories - women generally replace the earlier, male Lawrence - figure as representations of the searching soul (a development foreshadowed by the earlier use of Ursula in *The Rainbow*) - Kate is weary of life and, though she does not yet realize it, sick of modern society.

In Mexico City she meets Don Ramon Carrasco and his friend, Don Cipriano Viedma, the leaders of a new politico - religious movement which has as its object the overthrow of the

Catholic Church and the established government of Mexico, and the substitution of a new official government and religion based on the old Aztec gods of the Mexican people. Intrigued by this strange pair (she knows little of their movement as yet), Kate goes to live near Don Ramon, the founder of the movement, by a lake where she has heard that "Quetzalcoatl's men," as they call themselves, are particularly active. There she is brought into regular contact with Don Cipriano and the two eventually fall in love, if their idealized Lawrentian relationship - based on the kind of mystical, impersonal sexuality the author believed in - can be called love. In the meantime, Don Ramon's followers are busy overthrowing the church and state of Mexico and, in various ritual ceremonies, substituting their own Aztec hierarchy for the old Catholic firmament of God and saints. Lawrence wrote a great deal of poetry, some of it rather good, as lyrics which were presumably sung on these ceremonial occasions. A typical example is this song of Quetzalcoatl:

I am the Living Quetzalcoatl. Naked I come from out of the deep From the place which I call my Father, Naked have I travelled the long way round From heaven, past the sleeping sons of God.

Out of the depths of the sky, I came like an eagle. Out of the bowels of the earth like a snake.

All things that lift in the lift of living between earth and sky, know me....

For I am Quetzalcoatl, the feathered snake. And I am not with you till my serpent has coiled his circle of rest in your belly. And I, Quetzalcoatl, the eagle of the air, am brushing your faces with vision.

I am fanning your breasts with my breath. And building my nest of peace in your bones. I am Quetzalcoatl, of the Two Ways.

Quetzalcoatl himself is, of course, the plumed serpent, a mythical beast who unites the heavens and the earth. The eagle's plumes represent the spirit, and the snake's body represents the flesh in a single integrated being such as Lawrence believed a man should be.

When Don Ramon and company have succeeded in setting up their new system, the leaders play the parts of gods in official ceremonies, Don Ramon himself taking the role of Quetzalcoatl and Don Cipriano and Kate Leslie are incorporated into the scheme of things as the war - god Huitzilipochtli and his bride Malintzi, a kind of goddess of fertility. But by this time the constantly reiterated rituals and ceremonies have become undeniably tedious, and the official, propagandistic state religion that Lawrence seems to be advocating seems not only rather appalling (to those, at least, who believe in the separation of church and state) but quite alien to the deepest beliefs of the younger Lawrence, who believed in spiritual freedom and responsibility for men, rather than mechanical obedience to a rigid creed or dogma. The book ends with Kate married to Cipriano, and Don Ramon (who has driven one wife to death and married another in some of the more dramatic sections of the book) advising her to decide for herself whether or not she should stay in Mexico and be a dutiful wife to her savage little husband. It is a rather disappointing ending, justifying much of Leavis' distaste. Yet, as Tindall points out, there are so many splendidly barbaric passages, and so many scenes of both vividly imagined fantasy and vividly depicted Mexican reality that this great Lawrentian fairy tale cannot be entirely ignored.

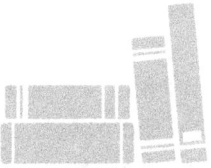

ESSAY QUESTIONS AND ANSWERS

....

Question: What is the relation between *Sons and Lovers* and Lawrence's own life?

Answer: As we have seen throughout the Detailed Summary, Introduction and Commentary, *Sons and Lovers* is for the most part a very accurate record of D. H. Lawrence's own early life. Mrs. Morel, we have noted, is a strikingly detailed and dramatic portrait of Lawrence's own, ex - schoolteacher mother, Lydia Beardsall Lawrence, and the hard - drinking Walter Morel, so bitterly hated by his children, is a vivid portrait of the equally - hated Arthur Lawrence, the author's father, who, like Morel, was a coal miner with a glossy black beard that had probably never been shaved. Miriam, as we have seen, is a fairly precise, sometimes rather unflattering characterization of young "Bert" Lawrence's first girlfriend, Jessie Chambers. Like her counterpart in the book she is an intensely religious, spirited girl who provided the budding writer with the kind of enthusiastic encouragement he needed to get started on a literary career. Annie is Lawrence's sister Ada. William is his older brother "Ern," who, like William, died at an early age of combined pneumonia and erysipelas.

The rest of the characters are a little more difficult to place, however, for once Paul Morel - Bert Lawrence leaves the sheltering cocoon of Bestwood - Eastwood, the one - to - one correspondence of life and the novel ceases to be so exact. Paul Morel works at Jordan's for about three years, but D. H. Lawrence only worked at a similar surgical appliance factory for one summer. Paul Morel early distinguishes himself as a painter, but Lawrence, an amateur painter too, won his chief recognition as a writer. Paul Morel's affair with Clara, which occupies the last third of the book, is perhaps the least autobiographical element, for it is not definitely known whether Lawrence himself had any such experience. Biographers suspect that he had an intense affair with a married woman in Eastwood, one Alice Dax, when he was around the age that Paul is in the book during his affair with Clara. But Clara Dawes is a combination of the qualities of several other women in the young author's life, chief among them being Louie Burrows, his one - time fiancee, and Frieda von Richthofen Weekley Lawrence, his wife. The death of Mrs. Morel from cancer, however, is almost an exact account of the death of Lawrence's own mother. And the despair and desolation felt by Paul Morel after this event is surely the same despair that Lawrence himself felt when Lydia Lawrence died (cf. the "Mother" poems is Collected Poems). As for Paul Morel's final reawakening to life, in the last paragraph of *Sons and Lovers*, we know that Lawrence himself must have re - awakened to life in the same way, otherwise where would he have gotten the courage and the vitality he needed to write *Sons and Lovers*?

Question: How does Lawrence depict industrialism in *Sons and Lovers*?

Answer: Although he had not yet postulated the clear - cut philosophical opposition between "the mechanical will" and the life principle as that on which a book life, say, *Women in Love* is based, Lawrence had already begun, in *Sons and Lovers*, to perceive and depict the evils which industrialism has wrought in modern society. A character like Walter Morel, for instance, has plainly been a victim of the mechanical, ugly world of the collieries and the factories, a world which leaves him only the pub and the pit for, respectively, recreation and occupation. There is no color, no organic rhythm, no vital ritual in Walter Morel's life. His days are spent in the unnatural blackness of the mine, filthy, sweaty and full of danger. His nights are spent pointlessly drinking and brutalizing himself with alcohol, in the local tavern. No dramatic diversions are open to him, no folk arts or crafts flower naturally from the context of his daily life. The efficient, impersonal mining company cares little for him and his needs: they house him and his family along an alley of ashpits. The community cares less: it provides no new opportunities for his children; their only way of "rising" in the world can be through occupations as mindless as their father's -soul - destroying clerking or exhausting, brutalizing school - teaching.

Two other obvious "victims" of industrialism are Clara Dawes and her husband Baxter. Clara, in the scene in which Paul visits her at her mother's house, is shown doing "sweated" work. This is lacemaking, which is farmed out to women by the piece to do at home at a criminally low rate of pay. Even Paul himself - less conscious of the horrors of industrialism than Lawrence as a writer was to become - is shocked at the thought of that beautiful, "superb" body of Clara's, that proud, independent spirit of hers, humbly bowed to the impersonal efficiency and power of a machine. Clara, who might have become so much, so ripe and splendid a person, is nearly destroyed by the factory society in which she must live and work. Baxter Dawes, too, a man who might have done better things, is, like Walter Morel, turned into a brute, a drunkard and a bully by the pointless, rootless world in which he finds himself. He is a failure in the factory and, in part for this reason, a failure in his marriage.

Finally, the experiences of Paul Morel, all of them useful enough to the young artist, nevertheless reveal indirectly the hardships and inequities of late nineteenth - century industrial society. Obviously superior, talented, sensitive, and artistic, Paul must, despite his extraordinary abilities, go to work as a clerk in a surgical appliance factory at the age of fourteen! He must leave "the beloved home valley" and feel the "prison of industrialism" - the long hours, the drab surroundings - close gradually in on him. Though he is relatively "happy" at Jordan's, chiefly in the sense that he makes some friends in the place, it is significant that he becomes seriously ill several times in the course of his career there. It is not just that he is "delicate" or sickly; he becomes ill because the dreary industrial routine is simply more than the flesh - or the soul - can bear.

Lawrence treated industrialism much more consciously and fully in many of his later works. For such fully worked out analyses of industrial society, the reader is referred especially to *The Rainbow*, *Women in Love*, (cf. the Brief Summaries and Comments included earlier), and *Lady Chatterley's Lover*, which contains a number of famous passages inveighing against the ugliness and soullessness of the industrial Midlands in which it (like *Sons and Lovers*, *The Rainbow* and *Women in Love*) is set.

Question: What use does *Sons and Lovers* make of the Oedipus complex?

Answer: The Oedipus complex, whether consciously or unconsciously used by Lawrence, provides the central action of this book. Actually we know, as we have noted before, that Lawrence was quite well aware, through Frieda, of Freud's theories about the Oedipus complex at the time he wrote *Sons and Lovers*. And there is surely no doubt that, as Graham Hough points out, the novel is based on "the Freudian Oedipal imbroglio in classic form." Mrs. Morel, as we have commented, seems to have a kind of "Jocasta complex" towards her two favorite sons, William and Paul. As Lawrence's letter to Garnett notes, she deliberately directs all her passions - disappointed in her marriage to Walter Morel - toward urging them on to success in life. Her passionate, intense attachment for them, however, arouses a reciprocal, and unhealthy, dependence in her sons. This furious love first destroys William, then threatens to destroy Paul, for it keeps the boys from being able to form wholesome and natural relationships with other women. They are not only Gertrude Morel's sons, but also her lovers, in the true Freudian sense. (Indeed, Lawrence himself recognized that he felt this way toward his mother when he told Jessie Chambers that he could never really love her because he loved his mother "like a lover.") Thus the book is actually an extended study of the Oedipus complex and its operations, an examination of the Morel boys' "neurotic" behavior as sons and lovers, sons and lovers of their mother, and unhappy lovers of other women. Again as Graham Hough has remarked, it is "the first Freudian novel in English."

Question: Why is *Sons and Lovers* a bildungsroman?

Answer: A bildungsroman is, literally, a "development novel," a novel which traces the growth of a single individual, usually an exceptionally talented and sensitive person, from childhood through adolescence to maturity. *Sons and Lovers* obviously does this and, as such, it is one of the most outstanding and most successful bildungsromans of our time. Not only does it show us Paul Morel at almost every stage of his young life, but it also familiarizes us so thoroughly with his home and his early social environment that we can - if we are determinists - understand and almost predict every phase of his later development. His childhood tantrums, the daily traumas of his boyhood (his father's drunken rages, his trips to the mining company office to pick up Morel's salary), his intense attachment to his mother, his vividly depicted relationship with Miriam, and his passion for Clara all help us to see how and why he grows into the special, artistic individual that he does become. This sort of thing, this sort of exploration in depth of an individual's earliest experiences (and hence his profoundest motivations) is the sort of thing that the bildungsroman uniquely does. It is a "psychological novel," a "case study" which presents us with a complete individual, Paul Morel, in all his dimensions, as real and vivid to us as if we had lived through his boyhood next door to him.

Question: What was Lawrence's attitude toward sex throughout his work?

Answer: As we have tried to show, Lawrence was not the hedonist nor the morbid, sexually obsessed neurotic that many critics (including T. S. Eliot) have too often accused him of being. Sex, for Lawrence, represented the mysterious generative aspect of the universe, the universe's "unaccountable" urge to produce life and yet more life. When a man and woman were sexually attuned to one another, when they undertook the sexual experience with the right, almost religiously reverent attitude, it would leave them awed and astonished by the fierce, "incalculable" life energy of the world, an energy which they found within themselves but which, in them, was only a reflection of the larger, life - energy in all things. Thus, in *Sons and Lovers*, Paul and Clara are left feeling, "like Adam and Eve," an amazement and a profound respect for this mysterious power that has swept them "out of the garden" and onto the human journey. And thus, in *The Rainbow*, Tom Brangwen and his wife, whose sexual relationship is a kind of pattern of what the human sexual relationship should be according to Lawrence, live mystically attuned to each other through the magnetism of sex, "in contact with the unknown, the unaccountable and the incalculable."

Question: How does the organization of *The Rainbow* differ from that of *Women in Love*?

Answer: *The Rainbow* is a family - chronicle novel, built not on a system of simultaneously parallel relationships (as *Women in Love* is) but structured around a number of roughly comparable relationships which succeed each other, as it were, in waves. Thus *The Rainbow* gives us a sense of time passing, of time wearing away, and individuals ripening, maturing, and aging. When we first see Tom Brangwen, for instance, he is a young man, not yet married, alone and sexually frustrated. But before the book is over he becomes a grandfather and then, finally, dies. A new generation, in the meantime, succeeds his; his step-daughter Anna and her husband Will take the place of Tom and his wife Lydia. Then, gradually, they too are replaced, this time by Ursula Brangwen and Anton Skrebensky. Yet the supplanting by each generation is never abrupt, obvious or melodramatic. Everything happens gradually, as it does in life, giving us a sense - appropriate to the naturally rhythmic farm environment - of the natural rhythms of things.

Women in Love, on the other hand, is a masterpiece of parallel, "architectonic" structure. Lawrence sets a number of relationships going at the same time: Ursula and Birkin, Gudrun and Gerald, Birkin and Hermione, Gurdun and Ursula, and Birkin and Gerald. These, in the course of the novel, gradually work themselves out in a brilliantly inevitable way. By the end of the book things are fixed in a final pattern: We have gotten an overall, simultaneous view of the world, of the interaction between man and society in a number of different circumstances. Thus while the action of *The Rainbow* seems to be mainly organized in time, the action of *Women in Love* is temporarily simultaneous but organized in space.

Question: Discuss the primitivism of *The Plumed Serpent*.

Answer: Like a number of Lawrence's works of this period, *The Plumed Serpent* was quite consciously "primitive" in many respects. For one thing, Lawrence had read a good deal of anthropology, and, in this connection, a fair amount of such writing bearing on the religions and customs of the Aztecs. He incorporated much of this into his ambitious Mexican novel. Then, in writing the "hymns" for the novel -the hymns of Quetzalcoatl, Huitzilipochtli, Malintzi, etc. - he made an obvious and deliberate effort to simplify and almost archaize his language, so as to give it a strange and primitive flavor. But most important, his whole enthusiasm for "the dark gods" of the Aztecs, and for the "native" gods of peoples in general, was a form of "romantic primitivism" almost as Rousseau's enthusiasm for the "noble savage" was a form of such primitivism. Lawrence, rather like Rousseau, felt that there was a vitality, a truth to life, a contact with the real, powerful sources of life, that primitive peoples had, and which modern man ought to make some effort to regain. Of course, after a while he was willing to admit, too, that the Indians had their drawbacks. They were brutal, dirty, uneducated, and - well, primitive! Thus, Kate, in *The Plumed Serpent* can never wholly make up her mind to abandon Europe and its nervous amenities for the mysteriously vital and dramatic movement of Don Ramon and his followers, Quetzalcoatl's men. On the one hand, like Lawrence, she feels that by abandoning her over - intellectual, highly cultivated, egotistical, "white" consciousness, she will somehow get into contact with the "dark sun" behind the sun, the mysterious generative source of life; but on the other hand, she fears abandoning herself, fears the lack of control and the loss of reason that could come with such self - abnegation. Finally *The Plumed Serpent* ends on a "lady or the tiger" note: we think Kate will decide to remain in Mexico as the mindless, sexually flowering wife of Don Cipriano; but then, after all, she may not!

SUBJECT BIBLIOGRAPHY AND GUIDE TO RESEARCH PAPERS

MAJOR WORKS OF D. H. LAWRENCE

(For greater detail see Roberts, Warren. *A Bibliography of D. H. Lawrence.* London, Rupert Hart - Davis, 1963 and Nehls, I. 527-31.)

The White Peacock. London, Heinemann, 1911.

The Trespasser. London, Duckworth, 1912.

Love Poems and Others. London, Duckworth, 1913.

Sons and Lovers. London, Duckworth, 1913.

The Widowing of Mrs. Holroyd. London, Duckworth, 1914.

The Prussian Officer and Other Stories. *London, Duckworth, 1914.*

The Rainbow. London, Methuen, 1915.

Twilight in Italy. London, Duckworth, 1916.

Amores. London, Duckworth, 1916.

Look! We Have Come Through! London, Chatto and Windus, 1917.

New Poems. London, Martin Secker, 1918.

Bay: A Book of Poems. London, The Beaumont Press, 1919.

Touch and Go. London, C. W. Daniel, 1920.

Women in Love. New York, Privately Printed for Subscribers Only, 1920. London, Martin Secker, 1921.

The Lost Girl. London, Martin Secker, 1920.

Psychoanalysis and the Unconscious. New York, Thomas Seltzer, 1921.

Movements in European History (by "Lawrence H. Davidson"). London, Oxford University Press, 1921.

Tortoises. New York, Thomas Seltzer, 1921.

Sea and Sardinia. New York, Thomas Seltzer, 1921.

Aaron's Rod. New York, Thomas Seltzer, 1922.

Fantasia of the Unconscious. New York, Thomas Seltzer, 1922.

England, My England and Other Stories. New York, Seltzer, 1922.

The Ladybird. London, Martin Secker, 1923.

Studies in Classic American Literature. New York, Seltzer, 1923.

Kangaroo. London, Martin Secker, 1923.

Birds, Beasts and Flowers. New York, Thomas Seltzer, 1923.

The Boy in the Bush. With M. L. Skinner. London, Martin Secker, 1924.

St. Mawr: Together with The Princess. London, Martin Secker, 1925.

Reflections on the Death of a Porcupine and Other Essays. Philadelphia, The Centaur Press, 1925.

The Plumed Serpent (Quetzalcoatl). London, Martin Secker, 1926.

David. London, Martin Secker, 1926.

Sun. London, E. Archer, 1926.

Glad Ghosts. London, Benn, 1926.

Mornings in Mexico. London, Martin Secker, 1927.

Rawdon's Roof. London, Elkin Mathews and Marrot, 1928.

The Woman Who Rode Away and Other Stories. London, Martin Secker, 1928.

Lady Chatterley's Lover. Florence, Privately Printed, 1928.

The Collected Poems of D. H. Lawrence. 2 vols. London, Martin Secker, 1928.

Pansies. London, Martin Secker, 1929.

The Escaped Cock. Paris, The Black Sun Press, 1929.

Pornography and Obscenity. London, Faber and Faber, 1929.

Nettles. London, Faber and Faber, 1930.

Assorted Articles. London, Martin Secker, 1930.

The Virgin and the Gipsy. Florence, G. Orioli, 1930.

A Propos of Lady Chatterley's Lover. London, The Mandrake Press, 1930.

The Triumph of the Machine. London, Faber and Faber, 1930.

Love Among the Haystacks and Other Pieces. London, The Nonesuch Press, 1930.

Apocalypse. Florence, G. Orioli, 1931.

Last Poems. Florence, G. Orioli, 1932.

Etruscan Places. London, Martin Secker, 1932.

The Lovely Lady and Other Stories. London, Martin Secker, 1933.

Phoenix: The Posthumous Papers of D. H. Lawrence. London, Heinemann, 1936.

The Collected Letters of D. H. Lawrence. 2 vols. Ed. Harry T. Moore. London and New York, 1962.

The Complete Poems of D. H. Lawrence. Collected and Edited with an Introduction by Vivian de Sola Pinto and Warren Roberts. 2 vols. London and New York, 1964.

WORKS ABOUT LAWRENCE

Memoirs and Biographies. Suggested topics for term papers: How was *Sons and Lovers* related to Lawrence's own life? How much of a part did Jessie Chambers take in the construction of the narrative? What was Frieda

Lawrence's contribution? How much of his own experience did Lawrence put into *The Rainbow*? In what respects is *Women in Love* a roman a clef? How did Lawrence use his travels in his works - not only in his travel books but also in his novels and poems? Discuss D. H. Lawrence and "the spirit of place." In what ways did Lawrence's working - class background affect his style and his ideas as a writer?

Aldington, Richard. *Portrait of a Genius But . . .* London, Heinemann, 1950. A memoir and evaluation of Lawrence by a contemporary novelist and poet who was one of his good friends.

Bramley, J. A. "D. H. Lawrence and 'Miriam'" Cornhill Magazine, CLXXI (1960), 241-249.

Brett, Dorothy. *Lawrence and Brett, A Friendship.* Philadelphia, 1933. As the title indicates, a personal memoir by one of his closest friends and admirers.

Brewster, Earl and Achsah. *D. H. Lawrence, Reminiscences and Correspondence.* London, Martin Secker, 1934. Illuminates Lawrence's interest in Buddhism and the Etruscans.

Carswell, Catherine. *The Savage Pilgrimage.* London, Chatto and Windus, 1932. An early, pro-Lawrence biography by another one of his close friends.

Corke, Helen. "D. H. Lawrence as I saw him." Ren. & Mod. Studies (University of Nottingham, 1960). By one of Lawrence's most important girlfriends, the "Helena" of the early poems.

E. T. (Jessie Chambers Wood). *D. H. Lawrence, A Personal Record.* The early life of D. H. L. -including much of the central *Sons and Lovers* material - from "Miriam's" sometimes biased, but always valuable point of view.

Lawrence, Ada and Gelder, G. Stuart. *Young Lorenzo, Early Life of D. H. Lawrence.* Florence, G. Orioli, 1931. Memories of Lawrence's youth by his closest sister.

Lawrence, Frieda. *Not I, But the Wind.* New York, Viking Press, 1934. Always fascinating and often significant memories of their life together by Lawrence's wife. It also provides, as Ronald Draper notes, "useful insights into the nature of the woman who so profoundly influenced Lawrence's ideas about women."

Luhan, Mabel Dodge. *Lorenzo in Taos.* New York, Knopf, 1932. Sometimes untrustworthy but interesting reminiscences by Lawrence's American patroness.

Moore, Harry T. *The Life and Works of D. H. Lawrence.* London, Allen and Unwin, 1951.

_____. *The Intelligent Heart.* New York, Farrar, Straus. 1955. The single most authoritative and useful biography of Lawrence. No student of the author should be without it. (Paperback edition available.)

Nehls, Edward. *D. H. Lawrence, A Composite Biography.* 3 vols. Madison, University of Wisconsin Press, 1957, 1958, 1959. A useful collection of source material gathered from the writings and conversations of people who knew Lawrence well, and from writings by Lawrence himself.

B. Studies of the novels. Suggested topics for term papers: Analyze *Sons and Lovers* from the point of view of structure, characterization, style or **theme**. Do the same thing with *The Rainbow, Women in Love* or *The Plumed Serpent.* Compare the bildungsroman elements in *Sons and Lovers* and *The Rainbow.* Discuss the picture Lawrence draws of industrialism in the first three of these novels. Discuss the primitivism of *The Plumed Serpent.* Analyze the effect of the many passages of poetry in *The Plumed*

Serpent. Discuss the central male - female conflicts and relationships in all four of these novels.

Beal, Anthony. D. H. Lawrence. New York, *Evergreen Pilot Series*, 1961. A short, useful survey of Lawrence's work, with special emphasis on the novels and, among these, chiefly on *The Rainbow* and *Women in Love.*

Beebe, Maurice. "Lawrence's Sacred Fount: The Artist **Theme** of *Sons and Lovers.*" Texas Studies in Lang. and Lit., IV (1962), 539-552.

Draper, Ronald P. D. H. Lawrence. New York, *Twayne English Authors Series*, 1964. A survey comparable to Beal's, but longer and more detailed.

Engelberg, Edward. "Escape From the Circles of Experience: D. H. Lawrence's *The Rainbow* as a Modern Bildungsroman." *PMLA*, LXXVIII (1963), 103-113.

Fraiberg, Louis. "The Unattainable Self: D. H. Lawrence's *Sons and Lovers.*" 12 Original Essays (24-1960), pp. 175-201.

Hough, Graham. *The Dark Sun*, A Study of D. H. Lawrence. London and New York, 1956. An intelligent survey, comparable to Draper's.

Kazin, Alfred. "Sons, Lovers and Mothers." Partisan Review, XXIX (1962), 373-385.

Leavis, F. R. *D. H. Lawrence, Novelist.* London and New York, 1955. Probably the most influential single study of Lawrence's prose fiction to be published so far. Emphasizes *The Rainbow*, *Women in Love*, and the novella *St. Mawr* to the virtual exclusion of the author's other important works, however, and makes a number of idiosyncratic judgments about some of Lawrence's novels which may not be readily acceptable to certain readers.

Moore, Harry T. *D. H. Lawrence: His Life and Works.* New York, 1964. A revised edition of Moore's 1951 study (of the same name), this deals mainly with Lawrence's writings, though it provides some biographical information as background material.

_____, ed. with Frederick J. Hoffman. *The Achievement of D. H. Lawrence.* A very useful collection of essays which includes, among others, excellent pieces by Seymour Betsky, on *Sons and Lovers*, and Mark Schorer, on *Women in Love*.

Moynahan, Julian. *The Deed of Life.* Princeton, 1963. A study of Lawrence's fiction, especially perceptive on the tales.

Tedlock, E. W. Jr. *D. H. Lawrence, Artist and Rebel: A Study of Lawrence's Fiction.* Albuquerque, 1963.

Vivas, Eliseo. *D. H. Lawrence: The failure and the triumph of art.* Evanston, 1960. Groups the novels into failures (*Aaron's Rod, Kangaroo, The Plumed Serpent, Lady Chatterley*) and triumphs (*Sons and Lovers, The Rainbow, Women in Love.*)

C. Studies of Lawrence's ideas. Suggested topics for term papers: Discuss Lawrence's "theories" about sexuality, politics, religion, art, "progress," etc. with reference to one or more of his imaginative works and, if possible, using one or more of his general critical works to buttress your argument. Discuss Lawrence's "primitivism," his romanticism or his mysticism in the same way.

Eliot, T. S. *After Strange Gods: A Primer of Modern Heresy.* New York, 1934. Contains a famous (and infamous) attack on what Eliot thought were Lawrence's central ideas.

Goodheart, Eugene. *The Utopian Vision of D. H. Lawrence.* Chicago, 1963.

Goodheart, Eugene. "Lawrence and Christ," Partisan Review, XXXI (1964), 42-59.

Guttmann, Allen. "D. H. Lawrence: The Politics of Irrationality." Wisconsin Studies in Contemporary Literature, V (1964), 151-163.

Hough, Graham. *The Dark Sun.* (see above) Contains a useful chapter on Lawrence's "doctrine."

Kessler, Jascha. "D. H. Lawrence's Primitivism." Texas Studies in Lang. and Lit., V (1964), 467-488.

Panichas, George A. *Adventures in Consciousness: The Meaning of D. H. Lawrence's Religious Quest.* (Studies in Eng. Lit. III), Mouton: The Hague, 1964.

Rieff, Philip. "Two Honest Men," (Freud and D. H. L.) The Listener, LXII (1960), 794-796.

Spilka, Mark. *The Love Ethic of D. H. Lawrence.* A rather partisan account of Lawrence's "message," which traces its expression in his art.

Tindall, W. Y. *D. H. Lawrence and Susan His Cow.* New York, 1939. Often mockingly condescending but useful, because thorough and scholarly, examination of Lawrence's intellectual and ideological sources.

Tiverton, Father William. (W. R. Jarrett - Kerr). *D. H. Lawrence and Human Existence.* London, 1951. An interesting study of Lawrence's philosophy by a pro-Lawrentian Anglican priest.

www.ingramcontent.com/pod-product-compliance
Lightning Source LLC
LaVergne TN
LVHW011721060526
838200LV00051B/2991